The Rule of Love

The Rule of Love

Reflections on the Sermon on the Mount

KEITH WARD

daybreak

London

First published in 1989 by
Daybreak
Darton, Longman and Todd Ltd
89 Lillie Road, London SW6 1UD

British Library Cataloguing in Publication Data

Ward, Keith, *1938–*
    The rule of love.
    1. Sermon on the Mount – Critical studies
    I. Title
    226′.906

    ISBN 0–232–51824–6

Phototypeset by Input Typesetting Ltd
London SW19 8DR
Printed and bound in Great Britain by
Courier International Ltd, Tiptree, Essex

Contents

Acknowledgements

The Scripture quotations in this publication are from the Revised Standard Version of the Bible, copyrighted 1971 and 1952 by the Division of Christian Education of the National Council of the Churches of Christ in the USA.

Introduction

The 'sermon on the mount' is Matthew's narrative of a sermon preached by Jesus to his disciples on a mountain in Galilee. The sermon consists of various teachings and sayings which had been passed down in a number of early Christian groups. They were attributed to Jesus himself. We do not have his exact words, since he probably spoke in Aramaic, and we have the sayings only in Greek. But there is good reason to think that in these remembered sayings we have an authentic record of Jesus' teaching. The strangeness, the pungent style and the memorableness of the sayings bear the stamp of a strong and distinctive personality. It is to be expected, however, that the sermon as a whole, the placing of sayings within it and its structure, will bear the imprint of Matthew himself (who exactly the editor of this Gospel was, we do not know).

Many of the sayings can be found in the Gospel of Luke, and one can see differences of emphasis and interpretation there. Only Matthew places them within one connected sermon; and whereas Luke has Jesus preaching on a plain, Matthew writes that Jesus goes up on a mountain, just as Moses had ascended Mount Sinai. Matthew seems to mean his sermon to be taken as a parallel with the Hebrew Bible account of Moses going up the mountain to receive the Torah from God. But he points out that Jesus sits down himself and teaches the disciples. For Matthew, Jesus stands in the place of God and teaches with an authority greater than that of the scribes of Israel (7:28).

The sermon has a closely interwoven structure; it is meant to express the teaching of Jesus on ethics, on the way to live rightly. Matthew is not just trying to give a historical record of what Jesus said. He is setting down the moral teaching of Jesus, as he sees it, as he had found it in various oral and written traditions, and he pieced it together into one structured discourse, so that early groups of Christians could hear it and apply it to their own lives.

The sermon is used properly when it is taken as a guide for meditation and for moral self-examination. Through its words, God can speak to us, to exhort, to reprove and to encourage. The sermon, like the Gospel as a whole, presents a picture of Christ which was developed out of the experience and reflection of the earliest disciples. It expresses what Christ was seen to be, in the experience of committed faith in his risen presence. Matthew's Gospel was written within and for such communities of faith, and the records of Jesus' remembered life are reconstructed with reverence and care in the light of belief in his raising to life by God.

The historical Jesus is the matrix upon which the gospel records have been formed, as the writers reflected upon the life of one who proclaimed the character and demands of God with a force and clarity which was quite unique. We follow the pattern of their perception of God, as they responded to what they saw in and through Jesus. In meditating upon the sermon on the mount, people can today reactivate that vision, and find Christ to be still a spiritual teacher of immense insight and power. They can, if they have eyes to see, find him to be, as Matthew found him to be, one who speaks with Divine authority, the unique Son of God.

What I have written is not a scholarly work which investigates possible sources and traditions. Such works exist: I have used them and profited from them and I note a few of them in my very selective bibliography. I simply present a set of meditations on the narrative of the sermon as it stands in the gospel text. Each chapter is designed so that it can be used as a basis for meditation and reflection. Some questions are included as an aid to personal thought or group discussion. Though it obviously does not have to be used that way, the sermon on the mount readily lends itself to such treatment, since it expresses the most profound moral teaching and spiritual insight. It seems to go straight to the heart of Christian morality, and to show what a truly Christian life should be.

But of course all individuals bring to the sermon their own perspectives and backgrounds. No interpretation is final or infallible, and each may add a new angle of vision to a familiar text. One of the things that has struck me most about the sermon is the way in which it seems to call forth a personal response from each of its readers. It turns out, in my view, to be a very radical and liberating document indeed, which shows Christian moral teaching to be a very long way from the rather repressive, authoritarian teaching it has sometimes been thought to be. It is radical, calling all our accepted moral beliefs in question. It is particularly opposed to the 'morality of the religious', who jealously guard their moral superiority and judge all who disagree with them. And it is deeply personal, in calling forth from all who prayerfully reflect upon it quite distinct insights, in response to its teachings. It does not tell us what to think, so much as inspire and draw from us our own original response to the living teachings of Christ. In the sermon, Christ does not really give us precise and detailed commands to be obeyed. He draws from us the inner resources of moral discernment which enable us to see what love is and should be. It is not very surprising that a Jesus who taught like that should have been put to death by the very orthodox and traditional religious believers whose traditions he himself wished to uphold.

I have been a teacher of moral philosophy for much of my life. That is the interest and expertise I bring to the sermon. In my view its teaching can transform the whole idea of what morality is and of how morality relates to faith. In consequence, I have devoted some space in the latter half to an examination of the general grounds of morality, and the way in which Christian morality expands and transmutes them into something richer and deeper. The primary purpose of this book, however, is to serve as a starting-point for discussion, personal reflection and meditation on what is, on any reckoning, one of the most important discourses on morality in the world. For Christians, it is the most important of all.

The Structure of the Sermon

1   *5:3–12*   The Beatitudes. The Nine Blessings:
1   The 'poor in spirit' (Luke: 'the poor')
2   Those who mourn (Luke: 'You that weep')
3   The meek
4   Those who hunger and thirst for righteousness (Luke: 'You that hunger')
5   The merciful
6   The pure in heart
7   The peacemakers
8   Those persecuted for righteousness
9   Those whom men revile on my account (also in Luke)

2   *5:13–16*   The vocation of the disciples: 'You are the salt of the earth, the light of the world'

3   *5:17–48*   Commentary on Torah:
Jesus as the fulfilment of Torah. The Six Antitheses:
1   On murder (refers to Beatitude 7)
2   On adultery (refers to Beatitude 6)
3   On divorce (refers to Beatitude 6)
4   On swearing (refers to Beatitude 4)
5   On retaliation (refers to Beatitude 5)
6   On love (refers to Beatitudes 7, 8 and 9)
Summary: Be perfect as God is (Leviticus 19:2, 'Be holy as God is')

4   *6:1–18*   Give alms, pray and fast in private; do not be spiritually proud (refers to Beatitude 3)

5   *6:19–34*   Lay up treasure in heaven; have right views (sound eye); serve God, not Mammon; do not be anxious for tomorrow or attached to worldly things (refers to Beatitude 1)

6   *7:1–11*   Do not judge; examine yourself; do not drag the sanctified body into sin ('do not give dogs what is holy'); ask for spiritual gifts (refers to Beatitude 2, where mourning = penitence)

7   *7:12–27*   Summary of Torah: The Golden Rule.
Conclusion: enter the narrow gate; beware of false prophets; bear good fruit; do the will of God; build on rock (refers to Beatitude 4, the pursuit of righteousness)

1

Happiness

Seeing the crowds, he went up on the mountain, and when he sat down his disciples came to him. And he opened his mouth and taught them, saying: 'Blessed . . .' (Matthew 5:1–3)

In a recent very popular novel, *The Name of the Rose*, the author draws attention to the belief of some medieval Christian monks that it is sinful to laugh – because Jesus is never described as laughing, in the Gospels. Since they spent their lives in trying to imitate Christ in all things, they tried not to laugh either.

However much we may admire their faith, it is fairly clear that they made a terrible mistake. True, the sentence, 'Jesus laughed', never appears in the Gospels. But he was said by some to be a glutton and a wine-bibber; he ate and drank with publicans and sinners; he turned gallons of water into wine at a wedding; and crowds flocked to hear him teach. It is hard to imagine him doing all those things (or even being seriously accused of them) if he had no sense of humour. Musical shows like *Godspell* have helped us to see how much humour there is in Jesus' parables and stories. And when St Matthew sets out to record his ethical teaching, in the most extensive account to be found in the Gospels, he makes it begin with the word 'Blessed', or, as we may rightly translate it, 'Happy'.

Happiness was something Jesus was very concerned that people should have. The chief gift he had to offer was the gift of eternal life, and I do not suppose anyone thinks that such a life is one of gloom and high seriousness. As the Psalmist says, 'In the presence of God there is the fullness of joy' (Psalm 16:11), and Jesus himself says that he gives a joy that no man can take away. Joy is one of the fruits of the Spirit (Galatians 5:22), a distinguishing mark of the life of the disciples of Jesus. I suppose it is just possible to be joyful without ever laughing, but I must admit it sounds rather odd.

Why have some Christians been so distrustful of happiness? Is it perhaps because the image of the cross has loomed so large that it does not seem right to laugh? Or is it the thought that laughter is out of place when one is considering matters of very great importance? But the cross was followed by the resurrection. The suffering of Jesus endured for a relatively short, though terrible, time, while his glory will last for ever. There is a place here for compassion and seriousness, but a much greater place for joy that death has been conquered for ever. After all, the fact of greatest importance for Christians is that they are promised eternal life with God; if that does not cause sheer spontaneous joy to arise in the heart, whatever would?

Happiness and laughter are perfectly proper Christian attributes, which Christ would wish us to have. It is very appropriate, then, that Matthew has him begin his teaching with the word 'Happy'. Almighty God is everlasting bliss, and what Christ brings to us is a share in the life of God. If anyone asks what the point of being a Christian is, one perfectly proper answer is that it is the way to eternal bliss and a sharing in that bliss.

In Matthew 5, verses 3–11, Jesus uses the word 'happy' nine times. But those who read the Gospels in the original Greek know that a rather special word is used, the word *makarioi*. There are other words in Greek for happiness. When the philosopher Aristotle began his work on ethics by saying that all men aim at happiness, the word he used was *eudaimonia*. Some translations of the Bible, including the Revised Standard Version which I quoted at the head of this chapter, try to make the difference clear by translating the New Testament word as 'blessed'. So this section of Matthew's Gospel is usually called the 'Beatitudes', the proclamation of blessedness for the disciples. The word 'blessed' suggests that people are blessed by God. They are protected and strengthened by God; they are healed and made whole by him; their lives are made fruitful and happy by him. Just as we might think of curses as bringing disease, misfortune and finally death, so we should think of blessings as bringing health, good fortune and life more abundant. The happiness Jesus talks about is a happiness given by God.

This is very different from many non-Christian ideas of happiness. Parents will very often say that they just want their children to be happy. They might simply mean that they want their children to enjoy themselves, to do what they want and to have a good time. That is perhaps why some Christians are suspicious of happiness – it sounds a little bit like selfishness. What if you are very happy playing snooker all day long, or lying in bed reading a book? How can that be the aim of the Christian life?

What Jesus teaches is that there is only one sort of happiness which is true, lasting and indestructible. Of course there are many things that people enjoy, which bring them pleasure. But happiness is something deeper than enjoyment. It arises from a very deep sense of security, from the sense that one is living rightly and not just filling in the time. It is quite possible for people to think they are happy when in fact they have no idea at all of what real happiness could be. Only the person who has known true happiness will realize what they are missing.

Think of two people who are deeply in love. Each finds continual joy in helping the other, in being with them and sharing in their life. If they meet someone who has no experience of love at all, but who claims to be happy, they will know that a whole dimension is missing from their lives. In the case of human love, this may not matter, for there are many other ways of finding happiness which are quite proper. In other words, that missing dimension can be replaced by others, which have a special worth of their own. One can, for example, devote one's life to the love of God or to the love of others in a more general way.

But Almighty God has created us so that all of us, without exception, might share in a relationship of love with him. Everyone can find something of this love, and there is nothing else in the whole of human life which can replace it. There is nothing else which can approach it for the depth and intensity of happiness it brings. So, while those who lack such a relationship to God may believe themselves to be happy, they are missing the very greatest sort of happiness human life can bring.

So 'blessedness' is not just a piece of good fortune which happens to be given to us by God. It consists in a relationship of love with God himself. It is a sort of happiness which lies in sharing in God's love. That is very different from just enjoying oneself by having a good time. The most basic difference between them is that one sort of happiness is centred on the individual self and its own desires, while the other sort of happiness is centred on God and his nature and purpose.

Jesus' message is clear. Anyone who puts self first will fail to find true happiness (Luke 9:24). Those who seek to centre all their attention on God will share in true and everlasting blessedness. And the simple reason is this: God has made us for himself, to share in his love. In realizing God's purpose for us we discover what it is to be truly happy. For we realize God's purpose when we are flooded by his love, a love that nothing can ever defeat or take from us. That is his greatest blessing to us, and the true ultimate aim of every human life.

God is the supremely perfect being; he contains in himself unlimited knowledge and bliss. He does not *need* to create a universe, as if there is something lacking in him. But it is the Divine nature, as the life of Jesus shows, to be overflowing in its goodness. God can create conscious beings who are different from himself. Why should he do so? Because then the supreme goodness and happiness which he enjoys can be experienced by created beings who would otherwise not have existed.

It is very appropriate to speak of God, as Jesus did, as 'Father', because creating finite agents is rather like having children. If we have children, then we have, by God's will, brought into being new souls who can find love and happiness. Each one will live a quite unique life, and experience a particular sort of happiness that no one else ever can in quite the same way. One good reason for having children is simply that it increases the amount of good and happiness in the world. So it is with God's creation. He does not create human souls out of any need in himself. He creates them so that there will be unique sorts of love and happiness, which would otherwise not have existed. God is the Father of all, creating distinct individuals who can have their own unique and worthwhile sort of happiness by their relation to each other and to him.

Jesus shows that God offers even more than this. He shows that God entered into the world he had made and took human nature into his very self. When God united Divine and human nature in Jesus, he made human nature holy. When it is united to God, it becomes part of God himself. So, as we become one with Christ, by joining his body, the Church, we are made sharers in the Divine nature. This may be in a very partial way, but it is real none the less. In Christ, we are taken into the very life of God.

Human creatures not only have a unique happiness of their own, which is a faint image of God's eternal beatitude. They actually share in God's happiness. They do this by being taken into a loving relationship with God. In that relationship, human and Divine intermingle and interpenetrate one another, until at last each of us will become fully conscious of the presence of God and each of us will be a perfected instrument of God's love.

Jesus thus shows us nothing less than the ultimate purpose of creation – which is that all things should be united in God (Ephesians 1:10) by being brought into the love of God. God's purpose in creation is that all things should be bound together in love. Thereby all created conscious beings will realize a unique happiness of their own, a happiness which will be completed by sharing in the happiness and goodness of God.

The longing for happiness which all people have is a natural and God-created thing. The trouble is that when people try to gain happiness without reference to God, they cut themselves off from the source of real happiness. To see that happiness comes from sharing the lives of others in love is to gain a glimpse of the highest spiritual truth. But that truth is only seen completely when we recognize that we are offered a share in the life of God himself. There is an indestructible and infinite love, which will never change or fade. When that vision comes, our idea of happiness is enriched enormously. It becomes, not solitary enjoyment, but the joy of sharing in endless love. That is the message Jesus brings. His rising from death confirms and validates it. How appropriate it is, then, that the sermon on the mount should begin with a word which should be the keynote of every Christian life, 'Happy'.

Questions

1   Have I really taken hold of 'the joy which no man can take away' (John 16:22)? Does my faith in the promise of more abundant life with God fill me with happiness? Can others see this happiness in me?
2   Is there a difference between 'blessedness' and 'happiness'? Is the search for happiness self-centred?
3   What does the Bible tell us about God's purpose in creation? What are the special and unique things about my life which God wants me to realize?

2

Non-Attachment

'Blessed are those who mourn, for they shall be comforted.'
(Matthew 5:4)

The Christian faith is full of paradoxes. That is because ordinary human thought is not properly equipped to cope with the mystery and majesty of God. All one-sided views fail to grasp properly the message of God's promise. So we continually have to correct our ideas by seeing how they are in danger of becoming one-sided.

This is particularly true when we think, quite rightly, that happiness is the aim of the Christian life. For when we see that happiness lies in accepting the love of God, it is easy just to relax and be contented in a cosy little world where all is secure and well provided for. Religion itself can become cosy, always giving us the music we like, the sorts of services that appeal to us, and the sorts of sermons we prefer to hear. When things are going well for us, it is all too easy to think that God is in his heaven, and all is right with the world. Happiness becomes self-satisfaction. Without our noticing, faith can degenerate into religiosity, the evocation of lovely feelings and a cosy personal relationship with a rather undemanding God.

That is when the teaching of Jesus brings us up with a jerk. It is true that he not only promises us happiness; he commands us to be happy. But when he tells us what sort of people are truly happy, it can come as quite a shock. 'Blessed are those who mourn', he says – which is like saying 'Happy are the sad'. In fact, in Luke's Gospel, Jesus says 'Blessed are you that weep now', which brings out the paradox even more clearly. To understand it, we have to set it in the whole context of Jesus' teaching.

Jesus is not making the silly remark that if a loved one has just died, you will be very happy. We have to ask: what are we to mourn for, and why? The clue is given by a passage in the Book of Daniel (9:20 and 10:2). 'In those days', says Daniel, 'I was mourning for three weeks. I ate no delicacies, no meat or wine entered my mouth, nor did I anoint myself at all.' What he was doing was fasting in penitence for 'my sin and the sin of my people Israel'. Mourning means grieving for sin, for the separation from God's love which makes the world so full of suffering and despair. Mourning is an expression of sadness and desolation, because of the loss of someone you love. The great and inconsolable loss that affects all human beings is the loss of God. That is the primal loss, which nothing can ever compensate for. So we mourn the emptiness of a world without God. We grieve for the hollowness of human life without the love which is its source and origin.

But what good will this grieving do? Will it not just lead us to despair? It might, if there was no remedy, no release, no reconciliation with God. But in fact the clear perception of the hopelessness of all things without God may be precisely what leads us back to him. What we see is a world which has rejected love, because love required the glad giving-up of self to another. Human beings choose to be ignorant of this rejected love, and to inhabit a world constructed by their own selfish desires. It is therefore a world of conflict and hatred, of indifference and fear. It is ruled by greed, hatred and self-deception. Locked in its self-destructive course, it is experienced as a world of suffering and spiritual desolation. In such a world, the beginning of spiritual insight is to recognize that the course of this world is bound to endless grief. In such a world, happiness can be little more than the refusal to recognize the enormity of suffering, the determination to ignore it or to minimize its consequences by erecting protective barriers around oneself.

The human world is slowly destroying itself by greed and conflict, but few see the inevitable consequence of human actions. Those who do will rightly mourn, both for the loss of the sense of God and for the coming destruction of so many good things. How will they mourn? By prayer and fasting; that is, by seeking to give up attachment to selfish desires, by seeing that desire for the things of the world without God is empty and vain.

It is not that the world is evil. The world is created by God for our enjoyment and for its intrinsic value. Yet we must voluntarily give up many good things, because our distorted desires may be trapped by them into a whirlpool of selfishness, which sucks us down deeper and deeper. When Jesus' opponents accused his disciples of not fasting, he said that they could not fast while the bridegroom was with them. But when he had left them, then they would fast (Matthew 9:14–17). So Jesus gave his support to the idea of fasting, as a way of learning to give up attachment to the things which increase selfishness. Fasting does not just mean giving up food. It means giving up whatever binds up to the world. It means giving up anything that we want to own and possess for ourselves alone.

This may all seem to be very miserable. We are to grieve for the vanity of life, and to give up lots of good things. It does sound as if we will be going about with long faces and grave expressions. Some people think that Christians *should* always be mournful and depressed. But Jesus specifically rules this out: 'When you fast, do not look dismal, like the hypocrites' (Matthew 6:16). There is no need to look dismal, because renunciation of attachment is in fact the best way to lasting happiness. Jesus says: 'Happy are those who mourn, for they shall be comforted.'

When we see that the world without God is empty, and when we give up attachment to selfish desires, we are liberated into a wider and freer state of being. We achieve that state by trying to empty ourselves of self and open ourselves to God. Then we are able to receive the gift which God sends, which fills up our emptiness. 'I will pray the Father, and he will give you another Counsellor, to be with you for ever, even the Spirit of truth' (John 14:15).

We are comforted by the one who is the Paraclete, the Comforter, who strengthens and fills us with the presence of God, until we can at last say 'No longer I live, but Christ lives in me' (Galatians 2:20). Now we see the depth of Jesus' teaching that those who mourn are truly happy. Those who snatch at transient enjoyments on the way to destruction are not truly happy. Those who see that selfish desire is what leads to destruction, who see the emptiness of the world without the love of God, and who seek to disengage themselves from all that feeds the self and makes it grow – they are the happy ones. For it is to them that God is able to come, to make his home in their hearts, to fill them with a joy that no one can take away (John 16:22).

The point of paradox is to show that the deepest truths of human living are subtle, complex and surprising. It is in giving up all things that we possess the world. It is in mourning that we find supreme happiness. How can these things be? Because the weakness, the giving-up and the mourning are not the last word. They are ways of tearing down the veils of greed, attachment and ignorance which bind us to the world. They are ways of opening up the world to the transcendent reality of God. They are ways of allowing love to take shape in a world which fears and rejects it. We might say that these are the forms and shapes of love in a world of hatred.

These themes are taken up again in the sixth section of the sermon, in Matthew 7:1–11. There is a danger that, when the world is seen as estranged from God, one might simply try to leave the world altogether, regard oneself as one of the chosen and pass negative judgement on the world as a cesspit of vice and temptation. Jesus' response to such a danger is very clear: 'Judge not.' In the Lord's Prayer he warns us that we are to ask for forgiveness 'as we have forgiven our debtors'. God's forgiveness is not unconditional, as is sometimes unwisely said. It is conditional on our forgiving others. A similar point is now made in another way – we will be judged as we judge others. If we judge the world harshly, we will be judged harshly. If we are merciful, we will find God's mercy. This may be called the law of moral reciprocity, and it is a central part of Jesus' moral teaching.

If we think we are keeping the moral law, or if we think God has chosen us for himself, it is all too easy to condemn those who do not seem to live up to our high standards. How easy it is to condemn thieves, prostitutes, murderers and libertines

– especially when we live fairly secure and comfortable lives. 'You hypocrite,' says Jesus. 'First take the log out of your own eye, and then you will see clearly to take the speck out of your brother's eye.' In other words, the battle against evil is real, but it is to be fought in ourselves. If we would condemn greed, lust and hatred, we must find them in ourselves and condemn them there. 'The world' is not somewhere else, somewhere we have safely escaped from. It is within us, and that is where our attention must be concentrated.

Jesus asks us to tread a very narrow path between moral indifference – saying that we must not judge evil, because it does not matter – and moral rigour – requiring the highest moral standards of altruism and honesty from everyone. He certainly never implies that morality does not matter. 'Do not give dogs what is holy,' he says. The wholehearted love of God and creatures which the moral law requires must not be tainted or compromised by motives of ambition or pride. The love which God gives to us in Christ is precious, and it must not be seduced by the 'unclean' passions and instincts which control so much of our lives. We 'give what is holy to dogs' when we take the human personality, sanctified by love, and let it be mastered by the passions of greed, lust and hatred. In this way, the 'pearl of great price', the Kingdom within (Matthew 13:46), is thrown to the passions of self-will, and those passions attack and undermine the human personality itself, making it bestial and corrupt.

It would misunderstand this saying dreadfully to suppose that we are, or possess, something especially holy, and that we are not to share it with others ('the dogs'). It is rather that what is holy in us, the heart of Divine love, is not to be left carelessly unguarded from the passions of greed and selfishness, which will seek to attack and devour it. The morality of love places its unbending demands upon us. Morality matters.

Of course, it matters for others as well as for us. But it is not for us to say what it demands of others, or to judge how they have failed to respond to the demands placed upon them. We must prevent harm to others where we can, and that may mean deterring and punishing those who cause such harm. We must carry out the sentences and punishments our law requires.

What we must not judge is the standing of each person's soul in relation to God. Other people may seem to fail morally in large and obvious matters. But it will undoubtedly be true that we also fail to realize the fullness of love which is demanded of us. So Jesus counsels us to judge ourselves, not others. However, if we recognize that this self-judgement will always be one of failure, that our best moral efforts still do not bring real love to birth within us, what are we to do?

In the sermon, Jesus' answer is simple and direct: 'Ask and it will be given you.' Once more, it is important to see the spiritual meaning of this utterance. Jesus is not expressing the naïve and obviously false sentiment that you will get whatever you ask for. He himself asked for the cup to be taken from him at Gethsemane, and it was not (Matthew 26:39). He is hardly likely to proclaim that the poor are blessed, and then say that they can all be as wealthy as they want, if they will only ask! On the contrary, the future many of the disciples had to look forward to was one of persecution, suffering and martyrdom. Jesus has just counselled his disciples not to care for what they shall eat, drink or wear. He is not now suggesting that they should ask God for such things. They are, rather, to seek first the Kingdom and the righteousness of God (Matthew 6:33). So it is significant that he now speaks of asking for bread and fish, the two symbols of the Kingdom of God. We must ask for the Kingdom, and God will give it to us as a father gives good gifts to his children.

Sometimes in the sermon it may seem that we are required to achieve supreme moral goodness by unrelenting effort, that the Jesus Matthew sees is a rigorous moralist, demanding all from us. But the sermon can only be understood as part of the preaching of the good news of the Kingdom, the supreme gift of God to his children. In Luke's version, Jesus actually says 'how much more will the heavenly Father give *the Holy Spirit* to those who ask him' (Luke 11:13). The meaning is the same as in Matthew's account. The gift of the Kingdom is the gift of the Spirit of God. When our love is exhausted, the infinite love of God is our only resource. So the hard edge of moralism is turned. Our recognition of our solidarity in sin with all human beings leads to true mourning for our human condition. It is precisely then, when we realize that we have nothing and can only cast ourselves totally on God, that the joyful gift of the Kingdom can become clear to us.

Turning the mind from the world when its emptiness is perceived may seem to be despair. But it is the way to the filling of the heart and mind with the unconquerable love of God. When Jesus teaches that those who mourn are blessed, he is teaching that when we are emptied of self, we shall be filled with the Spirit. That is the good thing which the heavenly Father gives to those who ask. 'For every one who asks receives, and he who seeks finds, and to him who knocks it will be opened.'

Questions

1 What does Jesus mean by saying 'Blessed are those who mourn'? What should I mourn for, and how can I do it?
2 Is this a world of greed, hatred and ignorance? Can I find these things in myself? What can I do to eliminate them from my thoughts and actions?
3 In what ways am I guilty of judging other people? Can I not find these same desires in myself? Can I learn not to condemn, but to forgive, my own neighbours and acquaintances?

3

Heaven and Hell

'Blessed are those who are persecuted for righteousness' sake, for theirs is the kingdom of heaven.' (Matthew 5:10)

Jesus teaches that the greatest happiness is to be found when 'the world', the realm of greed, hatred and self-delusion, is set aside and renounced. But it may be felt that for many people happiness is hardly a possibility. What about all those who are without food, who live in appalling conditions, who are tortured and imprisoned, or who are dying in pain and alone? Isn't it callous to suggest that they should be happy in their misery?

It may seem so. Yet Jesus says 'Happy are those who are persecuted for righteousness' sake'. Again, 'Happy are you when men . . . persecute you . . . on my account'. He is speaking directly of those who suffer for their faith, the martyrs who have so often given their lives to uphold truth, justice and their loyalty to Christ. Yet his words apply to all innocent sufferers, who seem to have done nothing to merit the pain they have to bear. In what way can they be happy?

It is precisely at this point that the Christian gospel of eternal life becomes so vital. Jesus says to those who suffer loss for the sake of what is right, 'your reward is great in heaven'. Some people find it rather disappointing that Jesus talks of rewards and punishments. It may seem a higher moral teaching to advocate that you should do your duty for its own sake, and not for the sake of any reward. Yet Jesus speaks repeatedly of rewards and punishments.

He tells people to give alms, pray and fast secretly, so that 'your Father who sees in secret will reward you'. He counsels us to 'lay up treasures in heaven', and he tells us that if anyone gives a cup of water to a disciple, 'he shall not lose his reward' (Matthew 10:42). Jesus speaks of punishments, too. If you do not become reconciled to your accuser, he says, you will never get out of prison 'till you have paid the last penny'. Again, it is better to throw away your right hand or to pull out your right eye than to be thrown into Gehenna – the burning rubbish-tip outside Jerusalem. He warns that 'every tree that does not bear good fruit is cut down and thrown into the fire', and that 'the gate is wide and the way is easy, that leads to destruction'.

Why should there be this stress on rewards and punishments? Would it not have been nobler for Jesus to have said 'Do what is right just because it is right, and for no other reason'? The German philosopher Immanuel Kant argued that if you make morality depend upon thoughts of reward and punishment, you really undermine it, because you turn it into a form of prudence. And there is something distasteful about someone who says 'I am *only* doing my duty for the sake of the reward, or to avoid later punishment'.

But Jesus never says that you should give alms *so that* God will reward you. He says that if you give alms, God will reward you – which is quite different. Of course, you should be truthful, just and merciful because it is right. But for Christians there is another powerful reason why you should do what is right: namely, that God commands you to do so. Immanuel Kant would have thought that was a terrible reason. Why should you obey the commands of another being, however exalted? Isn't it just infantile to obey someone else's commands – especially in morality, when you should be thinking things out for yourself?

Even though Kant was a great philosopher, on this occasion he has missed the point. God is not just some exalted being, who tells us what to do and requires unquestioning obedience. God has created us – called us into being out of nothing. He has done this in order that we should be able to share in his love, and find happiness by creating new values which we and other beings can enjoy. What he demands of us is simply that we become the sort of beings who are able to share in his love. His commands declare that we can only share in love if we first become loving people. We can only receive love when we are ready to give love.

So when we say that we must obey God's commands, we mean that we must follow the advice, the teaching, of our Creator, if we are to become the sort of people he always meant us to be – people who can be receivers and channels of love. That is hardly infantile. Indeed, it would be childish arrogance to think that we know better than our Creator what will bring fulfilment and happiness to all creatures. We should obey God's commands because they are the only way to our true good and the good of all God's creatures.

But are we back to prudence again? Are we only to obey God because it will pay? That is rather like saying that children should only obey their parents (assuming the parents are wise and loving) because it will pay. But the chief reason for obeying parents is that our parents love us and that we love them. Obedience is really a form of love. When we love someone, of course we will want to pay attention to what they say, do what they wish us to do and try to justify their hope and trust in us. Human children eventually grow out of having to obey their parents. They need to make their own decisions; and human parents are not always as wise and loving as they might be. But when we love God, we love someone infinitely wiser and more loving than we are. It will not be a question of consultation, discussion and mutual compromise, as it so often is in the case of human love. It will be a matter of free and glad obedience, precisely because the one we love is infinitely wise and offers us more than we could ever hope for. It is good that we should have to accept responsibility for making our own decisions. God does not give us the answer to every problem, or take responsibility away from us. There are certain basic matters, however, which God lays down as minimum conditions for finding our true good. It is a good reason for obeying God in these matters that he is infinitely wise and loving. However, the best reason for obeying God is that we love him above all things, and so we will want to realize his purposes in our lives and in the lives of others.

The difficulty is that we may not actually love God above all things, and we might be hypocrites if we pretend that we do.

Yet we do know, even from what we can obscurely see in Christ, that when we see God as he really is, we will love him as we should. In other words, the actual state of most of us is that we *wish* we loved God with all our heart and mind and will. So we set ourselves to obey his commands out of a sense of duty, hoping and believing that we shall one day come to obey them out of love.

If we follow Christ as our spiritual guide, it will be wholly reasonable to do our duty not only because it is right, but also because God commands it. We do what God commands because we have already begun to love him a little, and hope that, as Christ becomes more real in our lives, we shall love him better. As we come to love him more fully, we shall find ourselves better able to receive the love which he offers, a love which is richer and deeper than anything else we have ever known, and which brings a happiness incomparably greater than any other. That is the reward that Christ promises to us.

We should not think that if we give alms, pray and fast in secret, God will agree that we have gained a great deal of merit, and deserve a reward, a sort of divine 'Gold Star' for effort. It is rather that as we learn to be the sort of people who are genuinely charitable, with our hearts centred on God and not bound to selfish desires, we shall become able to share in the love of God. That is our reward – not a prize for obeying a set of arbitrary commands, but the true fulfilment of a life ordered towards love; the firm and final possession of a love which our free obedience has made us capable of receiving.

This is not a question of 'pie in the sky when you die'. That jibe suggests that we need not do much about the conditions of life on this earth, as we will all live happily ever after in heaven. It should be clear, however, that we will only be able to enter into the love of God if we have learned to be loving people. And that means seeking justice in society, caring for others and showing compassion towards all beings, so far as we can. If we do not do that, we effectively shut ourselves off from the possibility of love. And if we shut ourselves off from love, the teaching of Jesus warns us that we shall separate ourselves from God, from other people and from our own fulfilment. The word we use in English for that final terrible state of isolation, lovelessness and destruction of our true selves is 'Hell'.

There is no word for Hell in the New Testament. Jesus speaks of Gehenna, the public rubbish-dump in the valley of Gehinnon, outside Jerusalem. There the fire never goes out, and worms devour the corpses and the refuse which are thrown onto it. He also speaks of outer darkness, where there is weeping and gnashing of teeth. A great feast goes on within closed doors, but those in outer darkness cannot gain entry. At other times, he speaks of a great fire upon which chaff is burned after harvest, a fire 'prepared for the devil and his angels' (Matthew 25:41). The images he uses are of grief, exclusion and destruction. These are the penalties for failing to do the will of God, of failing to love with all our hearts.

The Gospel of Matthew contains many more references to this terrible state than any other Gospel. That possibly shows a rather sombre caste to Matthew's mind, which led him to emphasize this side of Jesus' teaching. Yet even in Matthew's eyes, Jesus does not preach a message of fear and damnation. He proclaims the joy of the Kingdom, and the idea of the 'fire of destruction' or the 'outer darkness' must be seen as a stark depiction of what a world would be like which finally rejects the Kingdom. The doctrine of Hell has been responsible for many corruptions of the central Christian truth that God is love and will go to the uttermost to save any soul from destruction. It would certainly be a corruption of this truth to think that God will torture us for ever because we have broken a few rules. The Gospel is about the health and sickness of the human soul. We find health as we become open to the love of God. We fall into sickness as we close our lives to love. The end of our sickness of soul is destruction – exclusion from the feast of Divine Love, and the disintegration of our selves by the fire of lust, greed and hatred. The end of that way is the complete destruction of the human person.

Jesus teaches that the easy way, which many follow, is the way to destruction (Matthew 7:13). He teaches that the way to life is hard, and found by few. To grasp the sense of this statement, we need to compare it with similar statements like: 'It is easier for a camel to go through the eye of a needle than for a rich man to enter the Kingdom of God' (Matthew 19:24). The disciples saw the implication – that rich men could not enter the Kingdom at all. And Jesus said to them, 'With men this is impossible, but with God all things are possible'. The point is that riches almost inevitably draw the heart away from God, and make it impossible for one to take the hard way of total commitment and obedience to love. Thus the rich exclude themselves from the Kingdom. The same is true of the religious, whom Jesus criticizes more than any other group. Their delight in rituals and pious practices can also be a way of avoiding real practical love, and so of excluding God.

It rather seems as if no one can enter the Kingdom at all. God, however, makes it possible by offering forgiveness to all who turn to him in penitence and faith. Jesus came, not to the righteous, but to call sinners to God. He compares himself to the shepherd who goes out looking for one lost sheep; for 'your Father in heaven does not want any of these little ones to be lost' (Matthew 18:14). Matthew's repeated talk of 'destruction by fire' cannot be understood without putting it alongside his parables of the Kingdom, which is freely given to the humble and penitent. Talk of Hell is not meant to be a prediction of what will happen to most people. It is a reminder of the ultimately destructive consequences of our failure to love. It is a reminder that love is not easy, but immensely difficult. And, when fully understood, it is a reminder that we can never love properly out of our own resources, but must turn to God and rely on him alone. Hell is human life without God, when it is clearly seen. The judgement, as John's Gospel sees more clearly, is not so much that God excludes us as that we exclude the love of God. 'I did not come to judge the world but to save the world,' Jesus says (John 12:47). And John elaborates on the theme: 'This is the judgement, that the light has come into the world, and men loved darkness rather than light' (John 3:19). The whole purpose in talking of such a state is that we might turn away from hatred and greed, and accept the gift of life which God offers.

It is misleading to think of God assigning punishments for demerits, in a fairly arbitrary way. Jesus is the supreme expression of the love of God, and he does not come threatening endless torture just because of a few misdemeanours. He does, however, speak in tones which are unmistakably severe. What he points out is the final state of anyone who ultimately and irrevocably renounces the constantly and freely offered love of God. As we embrace others in love or turn from them with contempt, so we fit ourselves, moment by moment, for heaven or Hell. The person who learns to love will enter into the love of God, and find eternal life. But the person who refuses love, who 'sins against the Holy Spirit' by finally turning away from the Spirit of love, will exclude himself from the love of God. There, in isolation and self-torture, he will enter upon a process of self-disintegration the end of which is eternal death.

It is unprofitable to speculate on whether there are any people in Hell, or how many there may be, or exactly what it is like. What we know is that Christ offers eternal life to all who repent and have faith. Jesus teaches that it is possible to lose one's soul, to lose eternal life. But he comes to offer eternal life to any who will come to him. He points out the terrible consequences of a life devoted to selfishness, and calls us to repentance. More importantly, however, he points out the unsurpassed joy of heaven, open to all who love God. It is in that sense that he speaks of rewards and of punishments, in the Gospel.

How does all this affect the suffering of the martyrs and of the innocent, whom Jesus declares to be blessed by God? It affects it most obviously by the promise of a life beyond death, in which those who have only dimly glimpsed God's love in this life may come to share in it fully. Of course we rejoice in God's presence and love now. But there is so much more of that love to be known, so much more of God to experience, that it is only natural to hope that we shall know more clearly what we now see darkly, as if in a dull mirror (1 Corinthians 13:12). That is a hope all of us may have. But how much more important it is for those whose lives are torn by suffering and pain. God is with us in our suffering now. But our suffering would be transformed if we could be sure that we should very soon experience a love and happiness that we can scarcely imagine. That is precisely the promise that Jesus makes. It is a promise which is very dear to all those who suffer for their refusal to commit evil or to betray their deepest loyalties. It is perhaps only the comfortable and secure who can scoff at the idea of rewards in heaven. For all who suffer unjustly or innocently, the promise of Christ that we shall be with him where he is gives hope and courage to endure all things, for the sake of love.

Questions

1 Is it right to hope for heaven and to fear Hell? What are the rewards of heaven, and how can we get them?

2 How can I obey God in my daily life? What does God want me to do today? Here and now? How can I show a vitally active love?

3 'I did not come to judge the world but to save the world' (John 12:47). Is Jesus the Judge of the world? How does he judge *us*, and how should we respond to his judgement?

4

Possessions

'Blessed are the poor in spirit, for theirs is the kingdom of heaven.' (Matthew 5:3)

When Aristotle wrote about happiness, he held that few people could ever be truly happy. For happiness requires good health, enough money to be comfortable, an attractive physique and good fortune. Only a few fortunate members of the aristocracy had a chance of those things, and even then they were at the mercy of disease and accident. So happiness was no more than a dream for most people, and an impossibility for women and slaves. Jesus turned this view completely upside down. He did not say 'Blessed are the rich'. He did not even say 'Blessed are the moderately wealthy'. What he said was an affront to every reasonable Greek: 'Blessed are the poor in spirit.'

In the Gospel of Luke, chapter 6, it is even more startling. 'Blessed are you poor,' says Jesus, 'for yours is the kingdom of God.' In Luke's version, he continues: 'Blessed are you that hunger now . . . blessed are you that weep now . . . blessed are you when men hate you.' Luke goes even further, and adds four woes to these four blessings, just to drive the point home: 'Woe to you that are rich . . . woe to you that are full now . . . woe to you that laugh now . . . woe to you, when all men speak well of you.'

It is possible to take these words in a superficial way, and think that Jesus is condemning everyone who is rich, full and jolly. Matthew sees the danger, and tries to avoid it by rephrasing two of the Beatitudes: 'Blessed are the poor *in spirit*,' he says; and, 'Blessed are those who hunger and thirst *for righteousness*.' Matthew is trying to bring out the inner meaning of these paradoxical sayings, without depriving them of their real impact. He seems to be right. After all, it is not true that God will reward all poor people, just because they are poor; or that he will punish all rich people, just because they have a lot of money. It is what you do with your poverty or wealth that matters. If you are rich, you must use your wealth in the service of others. If you are poor, you must not be filled with greed and envy, but commit your life and work to God.

Jesus is not saying that you should be satisfied with involuntary poverty, if you can avoid it. Just as it would be silly to think that God condemns the rich as such, so it would be silly to think that God wants people to be poor and hungry. Poverty adopted voluntarily is one thing. Not having enough money to buy food and clothes, when lots of other people are living in luxury, is quite another. The proper Christian attitude is made clear in the Song of Mary, recited daily in the liturgy of the Church: 'He has scattered the proud . . . he has put down the mighty . . . and exalted those of low degree; he has filled the hungry with good things, and the rich he has sent empty away' (Luke 1:51–53). God sends away the proud, the mighty and the rich. Those who lay up their treasures on earth, who are satisfied with their possessions and who keep them to themselves, close themselves off from the love of God. The poor and hungry – those who seek to possess nothing and are not attached to objects they own – are raised up, blessed and filled with God's Spirit, as Mary the mother of Jesus was, in a quite unique way. It is the attitudes of possessiveness and non-attachment that Jesus is concerned with, not the amount of money people have.

Jesus quite clearly contrasts the spiritual with worldly pursuits. In the fifth section of the sermon Matthew records four sayings on the topic of riches. 'Do not lay up for yourselves treasures on earth,' Jesus says, 'but lay up for yourselves treasures in heaven.' The heavenly treasures are the fruits of the Spirit (Galatians 5:22) – humility, mercy, the overcoming of greed and lust, the inner calm and peacefulness which is the mark of the person who has overcome the cares and ambitions of the world.

He makes the contrast even more starkly, declaring: 'You

cannot serve God and Mammon' (6:24). Mammon is the god of wealth. He represents all that money can buy – power over other people, privilege, fulfilment of all our appetites, and superior position. The person who worships wealth is one who seeks to own, to possess all things, and to dispose of them as he wishes. No one can tell him what to do. He has enough wealth to ride rough-shod over everyone who opposes him and to make others do whatever he wants. Given wealth enough, he can become a little god, surrounded by flatterers and sycophants, in total control of his destiny.

But, says Jesus, such total control can never be achieved. Illness, accident and death cannot be avoided, however much money you have. Worst of all, the person who seeks to possess all things, to possess the whole world, will lose his own soul. For all things come from God, the Creator of all. All things belong to God, and are only lent to us in trust. We are the stewards, the trustees, of the earth and all that is in it, and we will be called to account for how we have used it.

Matthew, in chapter 25, relates a powerful parable told by Jesus. When the Son of man comes to judge the earth, he will not ask, 'How often did you praise my name?' He will ask when we fed the hungry, when we welcomed strangers, when we clothed the naked and visited the sick and those in prison. For, he says, 'As you did it to one of the least of these my brethren, you did it to me' (Matthew 25:40). Poverty, loneliness and sickness are to be eliminated as far as possible, for thus we minister to Christ himself. If we do not try to eliminate them, we turn away from Christ, however much we shout aloud his name.

It is not God's will that anyone should suffer or be in poverty and need. How does it come about, then, that so many people suffer and are oppressed? A full response to this agonizing question is not appropriate here. It would involve a study of the conditions of human freedom, of the nature of the laws of the cosmos, of the integration of humanity into a closely interconnected network of physical and spiritual forces, of the role of chance and necessity in creation. But there is one clear and terrible truth. We ourselves are responsible for a great many of the very worst sufferings. God has created a world in which we can grow to fulfilment by sharing in his love. But where we can grow and respond creatively, we can also fail to grow and turn inwards towards self-pleasing. We begin to use other people as useful means to our own ends. We learn to ignore their discomfort and suffering. We even begin to take pleasure in exercising power over them, in causing fear and distress. Finally, we begin to hate both others and ourselves, as life begins to seem a circle of hatred and suffering. For, of course, others will treat us in similar ways, so that even the pleasures we get are mixed with the ills that the greed and selfishness of others bring upon us.

So much depends on how we *see* other people, on whether we see them as objects to be manipulated, opposing forces to be feared or as unique places where the love of God can be expressed. There is a picture by Magritte in which the world is seen, reflected in the pupil of an eye. It provokes the thought that the way the world is seen depends on the nature of our perceptual mechanism. We see what our eye enables us to see, and we see it in the way our eye determines for us. So, Jesus says, 'if your eye is sound, your whole body will be full of light'. If we see things as they truly are, if we see the things and the people around us as gifts of God to us at each moment, then we are filled with light. But if we see people as threats and opportunities for control, then we walk in darkness. The possession of great wealth can pervert our seeing. For it makes it harder for us to see people just for themselves, instead of as market opportunities. That is why there is always a tension between the worship of God and the concern to obtain great wealth. Money may not be evil, but the desire for it is the root of many evils, as it traps us in a circle of greed and envy.

In such a world, it is most often the innocent who suffer. The poor and the weak are oppressed by the strong. They suffer, not because they have done something wrong, but because they are victims in a society of injustice and indifference. God does not will the suffering of the innocent. But he does will that there should be a world in which people are free to love or hate, and in which the whole human community is bound together for good or ill. In such a world, many must suffer because of the sins of others, just as many will benefit from the loving help of others.

The possibility that suffering may occur is the price of creating a universe with creatures like us in it. The occurrence of suffering is the price of creating us. Is it worth it? In his novel, *The Brothers Karamazov*, Dostoevsky writes:

> 'Imagine that you are creating a fabric of human destiny with the object of making men happy in the end, giving them peace and rest at last, but that it was essential and inevitable to torture to death only one tiny creature – that baby beating its breast with its fist, for instance – and to found that edifice on its unavenged tears, would you consent to be the architect on those conditions? Tell me, and tell the truth.'

'No, I wouldn't consent,' said Alyosha softly.

Alyosha has no answer; but the answer is given in the central unspoken image around which the novel is built, the image of Christ on the cross. And in fact, Dostoevsky loads the case unfairly by supposing that the Creator of the world must find it essential to torture a baby to death, as a means to the happiness of all. No morally good agent would consent to create on those terms; Alyosha is right. But those are not the terms. Perhaps the key question could be rephrased in a way that puts it in a rather different perspective.

Imagine that you are creating a world in which all persons can achieve eternal happiness, but they are such that they can freely choose to reject love, and so hate and kill and torture others to death. They should not do so; they need not; it is not necessary that they do. But it is necessary that they should be *able* to do so, if they are to be truly free. Suppose that if they choose evil, those whom they torture will be avenged, and will be given overwhelming happiness, so that even the victims will judge it better to have been born than never to have been. Since they are free, you cannot know whether any of them will choose evil or not. Would you consent to create a world on those terms?

I think one might be more disposed to say yes, though still with some sense of dread at what may happen if things go wrong.

The question can be rephrased a second time: Imagine you create a world in which men may freely choose to torture others to death. If they make this evil choice, would you yourself be prepared to be tortured, in order to bring about the happiness of both victims and torturers at last? Now perhaps, if you had the courage and the love, you would not only assent to being born in such a world. You might plead to live and suffer in a world in which eternal happiness could be won for so many souls by your self-sacrificial act.

Now we have come to the picture of the Creator which Christ places before us. If God creates a world with us in it, and the worst happens, he is prepared to endure the suffering that results, to offer to all the chance of eternal happiness. The worst has happened. What was possible, though forbidden by God, has come about. In response, God himself has suffered on the cross; he has taken suffering into the Divine life, where it is for ever transfigured and charged with glory. From that time on, all who desire union with God must set their minds on that glory which comes by the way of the cross. If we desire fellowship with Christ in his risen life, then we shall also seek companionship with him in his sufferings. It is in that sense that the question is entirely changed by Christ. We are not asked to torture a child, as a necessary means to the happiness of others. We are asked whether we will stand with the suffering and crucified God. Alyosha's life is the unspoken answer to his brother's question. Indeed, any spoken or written answer at this point might seem irrelevant and perhaps hypocritical. To the agonized suffering of the tortured, Christ brings his own eternal sacrifice. In that silent sharing, the redemption of human pain begins.

God has created a world in which creatures are free to make their own lives and thereby affect the lives of others in their community, and their descendants. In this world, all things are intimately bound together, so that we cannot simply take out one part of the world and insert it somewhere else. We are parts of one whole, and we suffer and enjoy with one another. Thus it is that we, as the unique individuals we are, cannot exist in any other world than this. This world has been spoiled by the acts of our ancestors and of our fellows and we go on spoiling it by our own acts. Yet God has entered into our world, to unite it again to himself. We are called to share in this process of redemption, and thereby to affirm the world that God has made.

Jesus declares God's blessing on the poor in spirit, knowing that so much suffering is the result of our greed and desire for possessions. In a world in which so many are starving, it is not acceptable to live in luxury, keeping the gifts of God to ourselves. We need to learn to become unattached to wealth and possessions, so that if we have wealth we will not cling to it, and if we have no wealth we will not always be wondering how to get it. Jesus teaches that we should not be anxious about the future, about food, drink and clothes. For it is such anxiety which makes us cling to possessions and give them priority in our lives.

He is not teaching that we should not think about these things at all, as though we should be irresponsible and make no plans for the future. His teaching is that we must give up all clinging to possessions, the sort of attitude which measures status and position by the number and quality of things we have. Such an attitude will only lead to anxieties which bind us to the world and lead us to try to live as though we were independent of God. The poor in spirit are blessed, for they receive everything from God as a free gift. What Jesus asks is that we put God first. If we do that, there will be enough for all.

If we find ourselves asking why there is so much poverty and suffering in the world, the challenge of Jesus is plain. He gives no elaborate theoretical answer. He calls us to do something practical about it, and regard our possessions as held in trust for others. That is how we become poor in spirit. We stand with the crucified God and share in his work of redemption when we cease to regard things as possessed by us, and instead regard them as entrusted to us for the provision of the needs of others. This change of fundamental attitude is what is required to enter into the Kingdom of God. As we adopt it, the happiness of the Kingdom becomes ours. 'For where your treasure is, there will your heart be also.'

Questions

1 'Woe to you that are rich' (Luke 6:24). What does Jesus mean by this? How must I use my wealth and possessions, if I am to follow Christ? How can I make my business put people and not money first?

2 The Bible says that we have been made stewards of the resources of the earth. What can I do to be a more faithful steward, so that this planet and all its people can flourish?

3 Jesus died on the cross to redeem human pain. How can I stand with him, so that my life can help to bring good out of evil, instead of making things worse?

5

The Law

'Think not that I have come to abolish the law and the prophets; I have come not to abolish them but to fulfil them.'
(Matthew 5:17)

We naturally and rightly seek eternal happiness; but we are placed in a world of sorrow and pain. We know that much of this results from selfish desire, hatred and greed. We know that these are the things that must be overcome, if happiness is to be possible for us and for the whole world. But how are they to be overcome? Jesus gives an answer that may seem surprising. Perhaps people were looking for a radically new message, a teaching that had been wholly hidden from the world until then. But he says that he has not come to abolish God's revealed law. Obedience to that law is the way to overcome the root causes of human suffering.

Many Christians think that Jesus abandoned the Jewish law; that he taught a new spiritual way to God; that he put aside legalism and all the paraphernalia of Judaism. Matthew did not think so. He stresses that Jesus' attitude to the law is even more rigorous than that of the scribes and Pharisees. In verse 19 he says: 'Whoever relaxes one of the least of these commandments . . . shall be called least in the kingdom.' Every little mark in the Hebrew script will remain 'until heaven and earth pass away'. Jesus is a legalist, at least in the sense that he cares even about the smallest dots and commas of the law.

One problem is that Christians sometimes have a very misleading idea of what the law is. In fact the word 'law' is not a very good translation of the Hebrew word, which is 'Torah'. That word means 'teaching'. The Torah is the teaching of God, and it is found in two forms. The oral Torah is the set of principles, decisions and discussions handed down by rabbis for generations. The written Torah is everything in the Hebrew Bible (the Old Testament) from Genesis to Deuteronomy.

One thing to notice straight away is that Torah is not just a set of written rules. There are rules – in fact, according to one tradition, there are 613 commandments in the Torah. But these rules are set in the context of the story of the patriarchs, of the flight from Egypt and the journey to the Promised Land. The teaching of God is not only in the rules, but also in the stories, which tell of the dealings of God with the Fathers of Israel. Thus Torah has a much more personal feel than some arid book of rules. It is the record of the relationship of God with his covenant people. It is the record of a personal relationship, not of an impersonal rule-book.

Sometimes Christians are tempted to look at Torah much more legalistically than Jews do. We tend to look at the words on the page – usually in English – and try to take them as binding, just as they stand. However, a moment's reflection will show that this would be to misunderstand Torah completely. When we have laws written into a statute book, it is true that those laws lay down a set of precedents and principles to guide judges when they have to make particular decisions. But good judges never just apply the laws as they stand in the book. They take particular circumstances into account, and seek to interpret the law so that it meets new situations.

Torah is the living law of a people, of an actual community, the community of the Jewish people. So it needs to be interpreted and applied to new cases by judges – in this case, by rabbis. It may then not look very much like the original written law, though it will be based upon it, perhaps after much discussion and argument.

A good example is the law in Exodus 23:19 which forbids boiling a kid in its mother's milk. Many scholars think that originally this law referred to a magical practice of the ancient Canaanites, used to produce fertility. They think it was forbidden just as all similar magical practices were forbidden to the covenant people. Through time, however, that law has come to be interpreted as forbidding the eating of milk and meat dishes at the same time, or even on the same plates or in the same cooking utensils. It now plays a major part in the kosher food laws of modern Judaism.

How did we get from that original prohibition of a particular piece of magic to the large and complex body of food laws Jews now have? By a long, developing process of interpretation, expansion and codification of law by generations of rabbis. The law is not a dead letter, to be applied just as it stands. It is a set of principles to guide the decisions of the rabbis about how the community should so order their lives that they remember God at all times. Eating food is one of our most important and vital activities. It should remind us always of the goodness of the Creator. If we have a special set of food laws, governing what we may eat and how we should prepare it, this will help us to remember God constantly, in one of our most vital and everyday activities.

So the rabbis can develop the law to bring out a spiritual meaning, and try to make all the 613 laws point to that one great underlying law: 'You shall love the Lord your God with all your heart, and with all your soul, and with all your might' (Deuteronomy 6:4). But it should not be thought that the rabbis always agree. On the contrary, the Jewish tradition is full of the records of disputes among rabbis, as to what the laws mean and how they should be applied. It is often said that where three rabbis meet together, there are always four opinions. Torah is not seen as fixed in all its details for ever, but as always open to debate and re-interpretation. Of course Torah will remain; but as the law of a living, changing community, it is always open to interpretation by the 'judges' who apply it, the rabbis.

It is quite wrong to think of Torah as legalistic. Its rules cover the whole of human life, and serve as a constant reminder that God has made an everlasting covenant with his people, the descendants of Abraham. They are a record of the personal dealings of God with his people. And they are to be constantly reinterpreted and reapplied as principles for a living community. If we wish to understand Torah properly, we must see that it is a teaching rooted in the historical experience of one particular people, which they interpret as a series of encounters with, and responses to, God. It is thus historical, communal and developing; it cannot be separated from its historical context in the continuing life of the Jewish community. It is in no way individualistic, offering a purely personal morality which is none of the law's business. On the contrary, it is a social ethic through and through, an ethic for a political community. Moreover, it is exclusive to Israel and Judah, and is not meant to be a moral law for the whole world. It mediates a deeply personal experience of God, and cannot be rightly considered as just a set of rules for conduct. It is concerned above all with justice, with health, wholeness and integrity, both of individuals and of community.

It is this Torah which Jesus comes to fulfil. If that is right, his message cannot be properly understood in its fullness unless one has a right understanding of Torah. The study of 'the Law' should be a delight to Christians as well as Jews, and a common focus of their concern and reflection. It calls for a total devotion to God which seeks to make every action of life an expression of love and reverence.

The seventh and final section of the sermon stresses the rigour of Torah. It begins with the famous summary of 'the law and the prophets' – 'whatever you wish that men would do to you, do so to them' (7:12). That is certainly not meant to replace Torah, but to express its central concern. Torah is the way to life, but it is a gate which is narrow and a way which is hard to follow. The demands of morality which Jesus strengthens in the sermon are unrelenting. They are so hard that Jesus warns of 'false prophets' who will teach an easier way. True prophets will be known, he says, by their fruits; that is, by the good that they do.

It is not enough to sing the praises of the Lord, however loudly. It is not enough to speak oracles, to preach marvellous sermons, to heal the sick or to work miracles. There is one simple test of true faith, and that is that one does the will of God. Matthew's presentation of Jesus' teaching is quite uncompromising. Mighty works, inspired utterance and emotional declarations of faith are not enough. What is required is righteousness in action. Jesus says: 'Blessed are those who hunger and thirst for righteousness, for they shall be satisfied'

(5:6). If we wish to find true righteousness, then we must pursue justice and goodness in this life and on this earth with the same intensity as a thirsty man searching for water in the desert. That is the narrow way to eternal life and happiness. There is no other.

This may sound like a gospel of works; and we should not underestimate this quite distinctive Jewish emphasis on social and personal morality as the heart of true religion. Judaism has no thought of some religious state 'beyond good and evil'. It has no place for ascetic practices and meditations which are concerned simply with one's transcendence of the everyday social world. It has no great primary concern with correct ritual and special religious experiences. It is the most rigorous form of ethical monotheism ever seen, and its ultimate touchstone of faith is the purity of a moral life. Jesus presents this tradition forthrightly in the sermon.

Yet it also has to be borne in mind that obeying Torah is cleaving to God, and loving him with heart and mind and soul. It is not at all some sort of external conformity to laws. It must penetrate to the heart. It must unite the will so closely with the will of God that the two become one. In that union, obedience becomes love. It is that love, love which must show itself in action, which is at the root of Torah, the teaching of God, which Jesus fulfils in his own life.

Questions

1 What was Jesus' attitude to Torah? Why did the 'scribes and Pharisees' quarrel with him?

2 Is it important to study the Old Testament in order to understand the message of Jesus? Study some of the commandments of the Torah, and try to find out how they are interpreted by modern Jewish and Christian commentators.

3 Does Jesus teach that seeking peace and justice and caring for others is the heart of true religion? Are these the things I put first in my own religious life? Or do I care more about ritual or using the right words to express my beliefs?

6

Religion

'Blessed are the meek, for they shall inherit the earth.'
(Matthew 5:5)

Jesus, speaking to his Jewish hearers, reminded them that God
had given a teaching which required them to seek justice and
mercy, and to love and remember God at all times. He was
not talking just about the 'Ten Commandments', but about the
whole of Torah, the whole of the teaching of God for his
people. That teaching, he reminded them, was to be kept with
great rigour.

At the same time, Jesus taught that the commandments
should be interpreted and applied in a special way. He certainly
found himself in conflict with some of the teachers of Torah.
But it does not seem that he was rejecting Torah. Rather, he
was proposing a humane interpretation, opposed to what he
saw as a hypocritical and superficial interpretation that some
of the rabbis were giving. When he disputes with these teachers,
whom the Gospels call simply 'scribes and Pharisees' in general,
he does not say 'I don't care about Torah'. On the contrary, he
usually cites a passage from the 'law and the prophets' which
he proposes as a clue to interpreting Torah properly.

A good example of such a dispute is to be found in the
Gospel of Mark (2:15), which records that he ate with outcasts,
arousing the wrath of some religious leaders. But that breaks
no rule of Torah, although there is sometimes a tendency both
in Judaism and in Christianity to keep apart from sinners and
ostracize them. Jesus clearly teaches that one should freely mix
with sinners and outcasts – seeking, not to condemn and con-
done what they do, but to put them in touch with health and

wholeness. What Jesus could not abide was using Torah as a sort of boundary fence to keep others out – whether they are Gentiles, pagans, sinners or foreigners. We still do that today, when we think of ourselves as 'Catholics', who are really rather superior to other Christians; or as 'Christians', who are purer than Hindus or Muslims or whatever. In condemning such perversions of religion, Jesus can point to Torah itself: 'The stranger who sojourns with you shall be to you as the native among you, and you shall love him as yourself' (Leviticus 19:34). Obeying Torah should make you more open to others, more able to accept diversity, more charitable and kind to those who do not seem to meet one's own standards. It is true that Torah is meant to set people apart, as a people bound in love to God, 'married' to him until death. The temptation is to become 'holier than thou', and to separate oneself from 'the doomed world' entirely. Jesus points out, by his example, that Israel's binding to God is not just for their own private good, but so that they can be a 'kingdom of priests', a community which exists in the world to serve others.

A relationship of love exists so that it provides a strong and secure base for sowing love in the world. Love can never be self-satisfied, even when it is love between two people, or between a group of like-minded people. Then it becomes an extended form of egoism, and inevitably decays into group selfishness. This was always a temptation for ancient Israel, as it is a temptation for the Church. It is easy to love one another in a cosy group of lovely people. Jesus reminds us that love is mixing with 'publicans and sinners'. We are set apart, yes; but we are set apart for service, not for superiority.

Jesus' strongest condemnations, in the sermon, are reserved for the religious, not for atheists and unbelievers. In the fourth section of the sermon, an elaboration of the third Beatitude, 'Blessed are the meek', Jesus says: 'Beware of practising your piety before men in order to be seen by them' (6:1). Commenting on the three traditional religious duties of almsgiving, prayer and fasting, he does not say that they should be given up. But he does say very clearly that they should not be practised in public, in order that other people can applaud one's piety. When you give to charity, do not let anyone see what you are giving. In this context, it is ironic that the sentence, 'Let your light so shine before men that they may see your good works and glorify your Father which is in heaven' has been used just before the offertory in some churches. Giving money to the needy is precisely what Jesus told us not to let other people see! When Jesus talks of letting your light shine before men, he refers to the life of patience, love and joy which may lead people to give glory to God, who brings these things to birth in human lives. The corruptions of religion are subtle and manifold. One of them is the conspicuous donation of money and possessions to charity. More widely, it is the concern to accumulate merit by doing good works that Jesus seems to condemn. Good works *should* be performed, but 'in secret', and not to earn the praise of other people.

Similarly, he condemns conspicuous, long and repetitious public prayer. And he condemns any practice of fasting and voluntary renunciation which 'may be seen by men'. Why should these things be condemned? Because they are conducive to the most subtle and destructive form of pride, pride in spiritual things. Just as you can take pride in keeping Torah, so you can take pride in doing your religious duties. You can even do them more than most other people; you can be a spiritual hero and a public saint. Jesus' stern warning is that if you do set out to gain such a reputation, you will not inherit the 'land', the Kingdom and promise of God.

To those who regard Torah as a badge of exclusiveness, always ready to throw deviants out and to enforce conformity, Jesus must seem to be rejecting Torah. He certainly is rejecting that interpretation of it. But he gives a truer interpretation of Torah, as a teaching to give one the strength to love others, a badge of service and humility. Thus he does not reject Torah, but helps us to see what it truly means, and fulfils it in his own life. Jesus *is* the fulfilment of Torah. He is our Torah, the teaching of God; six hundred and thirteen commandments focused and vivified in the form of a living person.

It has often been thought that Jesus himself broke Torah, or taught that it should be broken. On closer inspection, there is no recorded instance of this in the Gospels. It may be helpful to look at some of the incidents when Jesus gets into arguments with the group of scribes who opposed him and eventually engineered his death. The Gospel of Mark, chapter 2, verses 23–26, recounts how Jesus and his disciples picked corn on the Sabbath. Mark 3:4 reports that Jesus healed on the Sabbath. And Mark 7:8–13 states that his disciples did not ritually wash before meals. These things have sometimes been taken to show that Jesus did not care about Torah. On the contrary, however, when Jesus answers his critics, he does so by reference to Scripture; and he does not say anything which has not been said by many orthodox rabbis from that time to this. None of these activities were forbidden by Torah, except on an unusually restrictive interpretation – that picking corn is 'work'; that healing is work; and that ritual washing is entailed by the purity commandments. Most rabbis would agree with Jesus that such interpretations are unjustified. The two great commandments are to love God and to love one's neighbour as oneself. When Jesus cites these, he does not abandon the rest of Torah; but he asserts that these commands must be the keys to interpreting all the others. In cases of human need, the Sabbath rest may be – and in cases of desperate need, it *must* be – relaxed. What Jesus protests about is the multiplication of religious rules and regulations, which are then used in order to criticize others.

It is a pity that the Gospels sometimes refer simply to the 'scribes and Pharisees' as opposing Jesus, when orthodox Judaism would largely agree with his attitude. Undoubtedly he was opposed by influential groups in Palestine at that time; but it should never be thought that all the Jews opposed him, or that he renounced Jewish belief. The basic point is that, when religious rules become excuses for condemning other people, and when they become means of parading one's own piety in public, they pervert their purpose. The rules must always point to the love of God. That is what they were designed for, and that is what Jesus teaches that they should do.

There is one case where it seems that Jesus renounced Torah. In Mark 7:19, some English translations have a phrase like: 'Thus he declared all foods clean' (Revised Standard Version). If this is true, then Jesus did reject the food laws, a very central part of Torah. Is this conceivable? A closer look at the Greek text helps to resolve this issue. In Greek, it reads: '*katharizon panta ta bromata'*, which literally means 'making clean all food'. The whole passage would then read: 'Do you not see that whatever goes into a man from outside cannot defile him, since it enters, not his heart but his stomach, and so is evacuated, making clean all food?' That is, evacuation makes all food alike, and it leaves no evil traces behind. Evil does not come from the food, but from the heart.

Jesus' teaching is that food does not make a man evil; it is the thoughts and desires of the heart which breed evil. Again, the rabbis would agree wholeheartedly with this. But that is no reason for giving up the food laws, which are meant to remind Jews of their covenant with God and make every meal a sacrament of his presence. It is the misuse of the laws he objects to, not the laws themselves. The point is slightly obscure even in Greek. But it is a plausible reading to take Jesus as saying that food which has passed through the stomach is no longer classifiable as unclean. In the public drain it is all one, and we can no longer distinguish clean and unclean food. So food passes through the body and is cleansed; it is not what truly defiles a man. At least this supposition has the merit of agreeing with the general testimony of the Gospels that Jesus kept Torah, and it does not involve us in having to say that Mark basically disagreed with Matthew about the quite important matter of Jesus' attitude to Torah.

It seems, then, that Jesus accepts the rules and regulations of the religion in which he was brought up. He accepts it as a valid Divine revelation. Yet he is keenly conscious of the misuses to which religion can be put. It can breed spiritual pride and hypocrisy, in the most subtle ways. It can provide the believer with a secret sense of superiority, and breed opposition and party-spirit by unresolvable arguments about correct interpretation. When he calls for 'meekness' or proper humility, he is asking us to root out even the most subtle forms of spiritual pride – the conviction of our own unique correctness, the awareness of our own spiritual pre-eminence – from our commitment of faith. Only when we have done so, when we are nc longer overtly 'religious' or pious in the sight of others, will we inherit the promised land, which is the Kingdom into which God calls us, a Kingdom in which 'religion' will no longer exist.

Questions

1 'You shall love foreigners who live in your land as you love yourself' (Leviticus 19:34). What am I doing to show such practical and effective love?

2 The Church exists to serve the world, to show Christ's effective love. Is this what my local church does? Is that how it is seen by others?

3 Do I use my religion as a way of excluding or condemning others? Does it help to make me proud (taking the 'chief seats', wearing gorgeous robes with marks of rank, parading my charitable giving in public)? If so, what am I to do about it?

7

Life

'Unless your righteousness exceeds that of the scribes and Pharisees, you will never enter the kingdom of heaven.' (Matthew 5:20)

Jesus did not come to abolish Torah but to fulfil it. He taught that it should be kept with even greater rigour than by the Pharisees. Of course, it should be interpreted wisely, in the light of the two great commandments. But it should be kept.

How can it be, then, that followers of Jesus today do not keep Torah? Many of us do not even know exactly what is in it, and we do not worry about that. How can this be?

The answer to this question is of very great importance for Christian living. It means that, whatever we may say, we do not think we need to obey the recorded words of Jesus, exactly as they are set down. He says: 'Whoever relaxes one of the least of these commandments . . . shall be called least in the kingdom' (5:19). But we ignore most of them completely. So we have to agree that there is no way straight from what Jesus says to what we must do. It is never a sufficiently good argument, in ethics, to say 'Jesus said this'. For we already ignore one of the most important things Jesus said, right at the beginning of the sermon on the mount.

This does not mean that we can simply ignore the words of Jesus. It means that there may be many other things to consider before we can know how his words apply to us. In this case, of course, what made all the difference was that the Church became a Gentile organization, not a Jewish one any longer. Jesus was speaking to Jews, and telling them that Torah would never pass away for the people of the 'first covenant'. All the apostles were Jews, and apparently they continued to keep Torah to the end.

Peter boasts of keeping Torah; he would hardly preach to Gentiles until he had his great visions at Joppa. In Acts 10:9–15, Peter stresses that he has never eaten anything unclean. The vision he has of a sheet descending from the sky with both clean and unclean food on it perplexes and troubles him. This is the strongest evidence that Jesus had not taught the apostles that Torah was to be abandoned, either before or after his resurrection. Nevertheless, Peter accepted that the Spirit was saying something new; the implication of his vision was that new Christians who were not Jews did not have to keep Torah, despite the teaching of Jesus.

It was Paul's success in bringing in Gentile converts that first raised the question of Torah. Were Gentile Christians to keep the first covenant? Or were they, as non-Jews, free from both the duties and privileges of Torah? Though Paul argued successfully for freedom from Torah, he himself apparently remained faithfully observant. Acts 21:2–25 shows him still keeping Torah, and being prepared to demonstrate the fact publicly, to avoid giving scandal to the Jerusalem Christians. The abandonment of Torah was no easy and readily agreed decision. The early Church evidently argued about it, and the first Council of the Church, at Jerusalem, came to a compromise decision, reported in Acts 15. They decided to give up circumcision but keep the food laws. Some time later, they gave up the food laws too. What happened, in other words, was that new circumstances – the flood of Gentile converts – caused the apostles to reflect on their new life in Christ and seek to apply the basic message of Jesus in a new way.

They saw that to apply the words of Jesus literally to a new situation would miss the whole point of his message. It would place difficulties in the way of new disciples, who had no Jewish heritage at all. They could from now on find their Torah in the person of Jesus. Moreover, the Church thereby assumed a creative role in moving to new understandings of what God required of his people. They were no longer to be bound by the written code, but to share in the freedom of the Spirit, to move to new and wider understandings of what love requires.

This does not mean that Christians can give up moral laws altogether. But it does mean something very important. Christian life is no longer to be thought of primarily in terms of laws, of a fixed code. It is to be thought of in terms of responding to a person, and sharing in the life of that person. For those who accept the new covenant which Jesus brings, he is the fulfilment of Torah, of all God's demands and promises. We are no longer to find the answer to moral problems by looking in a book. We are to seek to resolve our problems by responding to a person. Morality is transformed by the love of God, made intimate and personal in Jesus, and made known to us in the community of the Spirit, the Church which is the body of Christ on earth.

Jesus tells us that our righteousness must exceed that of the scribes and Pharisees. There is only one way in which this can be. We cannot compete in the matter of keeping the laws. We can only do it – as they can do it – by having in ourselves the righteousness of God, the perfection and justice and goodness of God himself. We will never achieve that by any human effort. It will only happen if God places his perfection, justice and goodness – in short, his love – within our hearts. That love is pefectly expressed in Christ, who has become Torah for us. So when Jesus tells us to keep Torah, he is imploring us simply to accept him as the perfect expression of Divine love, the perfect fulfilment of Torah.

That is why the Church was right to set aside the apparent teaching of Jesus, that Torah should be kept rigorously. For she saw that the inner meaning of the teaching was that the person of Jesus is itself the fulfilment of Torah. If we are united to him by grace – but only then – we are no longer bound by a written code. Paul, writing to the Christians at Rome, said 'Christ is the end of the law' (Romans 10:4). He is the end, in the sense of goal or purpose. But, having fulfilled that end in himself, he also brings the law to an end for those who are united to him in faith and trust.

What this teaching does is to put morality in a wholly new light. It is no longer a set of duties which we must simply obey. It is the attraction of the ideal person of Christ, which we are to embody in ourselves, and which we pursue chiefly because we love and revere and delight in it. The vision of Christ is the foundation of morality, for a Christian. That is why the keynote of the Christian life is not obedience, but enraptured love. We do not start from trying to obey; we start from seeking to see, from seeking to see God as he truly is. When we see him, we shall become like him; and when we are like him, we shall have passed beyond the stern voice of duty into the rapture of love.

But can we really find this teaching in the Gospel of Matthew? Many people have found, or claimed to find, a great difference between the teaching of the first three Gospels and the teaching of the New Testament Letters; between, we might say, Matthew and Paul. Certainly, the sermon as presented by Matthew can seem to be a morally rigorous document, demanding strict adherence to the law – and more; promising judgement on works and spelling out a very austere Christian morality of perfection. Jesus appears as the coming King of Judgement, the King of the world, a figure of awe, set apart from us by his purity. What is there here of forgiveness and atonement? Of the Christ who dwells in the heart and unites us to God by the free gift of grace? Was Paul's Gospel something new and strange to Matthew?

The contrast is more apparent than real. One might certainly expect that different followers of Christ would have differing perspectives on his life and work, just as different theologians do today. That is part of the richness of the faith, which speaks in different ways to very different kinds of people. But both Matthew and Paul (or the writers of the New Testament Letters in general) accept Jesus as the chosen one of God, who taught with authority, who was crucified and appeared to his disciples after his death, who reigns in heaven and who will return to judge the world. Both agree that, in the light of his life and teaching, all people are convicted of sin, of both moral imperfection and estrangement from God. We cannot read the sermon on the mount without being filled with a sense of our radical inability to live up to the ideals of love which it places before us. And that is just what Paul says when he writes: 'No human being will be justified in his (God's) sight by works of the law, since through the law comes knowledge of sin' (Romans 3:20). The motto of the sermon might well be the command, 'You must be perfect' (5:48). But it would be a radical misreading of the sermon to think that only if we are wholly without sin will we enter the Kingdom. That would hardly be a gospel – it would be the most depressing news we could ever hear!

What the sermon really tells us is that we can never hope to justify ourselves by good works. We might think we are morally good, that we have done nothing wrong. We might think that we keep the letter of the law. But Jesus strips that self-deception away piece by piece as he exposes what the law itself really requires. It does not require just not actually killing anyone. It requires the rooting-out of all anger and hatred from the heart. It does not require us to give ten per cent of our income away in tithes. It requires us to regard all our possessions as held in trust for the service of God. It does not require us to be kind to those we approve of. It requires us actively to seek the good of those we most dislike, to learn a universal and unrestricted love.

Not only does the sermon point us to an ideal. It inevitably brings to light the fact that each of us stands already under judgement – judged by our own failure to love God with all our hearts and minds, and our neighbours as ourselves. One cannot read the sermon carefully without knowing this. It undermines any moral security and self-satisfaction we may ever have had. What at first looked like a morally rigorous code of conduct turns out to be one of the most devastating exposures of human moral failure ever uttered.

How can this be? Did Jesus preach to depress his hearers? No, he never condemns; he never berates his disciples for their sins. He offers only blessing and forgiveness: 'Blessed are the poor in spirit, the meek, the merciful, the penitent.' For Matthew, as Jesus stands before those who hear him he makes the kingdom already present among them: 'If it is by the Spirit of God that I cast out demons, then the kingdom of God has come upon you' (12:28). And he says to those who hear him: 'Come to me, all who labour and are heavy laden, and I will give you rest . . . for my yoke is easy and my burden is light' (11:28–30).

This is not a stern judge who will only usher in the Kingdom at some future time. It is a man who bears the Kingdom in his own person, who calls men and women to follow him to find life and rest. So in Matthew's Gospel, Jesus does not just say 'Keep Torah; that is enough'. By showing what Torah truly is and what it truly requires, he makes it clear that Torah cannot be kept. But he does not condemn. He asks people, instead, to turn to him, to receive the Spirit which is his, to receive the forgiveness which he offers, and to unite their lives to his by leaving their old lives behind and following him.

Matthew sets the sermon in a context where it is preached to Jews early in Jesus' Galilean ministry. Its full meaning could not become known until that ministry had been completed, until Jesus had risen and the new spirit-filled community had come into being, who knew Christ no longer after the flesh, but as a living power and presence within and among them. Paul brings out that meaning, primarily for Gentiles to whom Torah meant little, and for whom crucifixion and resurrection were past events. He wrote in a context in which observance of Torah was already being abandoned by the young churches, and for which Jesus' earthly ministry was completed. Matthew records the young preacher, hinting at a fulfilment his hearers could not yet hope to understand. Paul looks back from the churches' experience of the risen Lord, and offers the mature fruit grown from that seed.

Yet Matthew knew that fruit, too. He wrote for a Church which also knew the resurrection and gift of the Spirit as completed facts. So, always standing behind the figure of the young preacher on a hill in Galilee there is the risen Lord of glory, giving to all the spoken words a deeper unspoken resonance. The words call to a greater observance of Torah. But the unseen Lord calls all people to him, where all failure is forgiven and desperate effort is replaced by rest and the gift of endless love. As we hear the sermon, we know that we stand under judgement and that we must live by grace, by the forgiveness and love of God freely offered in return for our penitence and trust. That is exactly what Paul says.

It is the death of Christ, still in the future as the sermon is spoken, which sets us free from the sin which the sermon exposes. With this liberation, Paul teaches that Torah is abolished (Ephesians 2:15) and Gentiles are brought into the King-

dom. It is not that we can now do what we like. God has still
'created us for a life of good deeds' (Ephesians 2:10). But the
risen Lord now becomes Torah. As Torah was to be set within
the heart, so now Christ is to dwell in our hearts through faith
(Ephesians 3:17), and we are to 'be filled with all the fullness
of God'. The secret of God's purpose, hidden until the time of
Christ, is this: 'Christ in you, the hope of glory' (Colossians
1:27). We are to bury our old lives with Christ, so that we may
be raised to a new life by union with him. Jesus' call to leave
the old life and follow him in the hills of Galilee takes on a
more profound meaning, as a call to die to self and be taken
into the life of the eternal Christ.

Now, says Paul, 'we serve not under the old written code
but in the new life of the Spirit' (Romans 7:6). There is an
immense feeling of liberation from all written codes (even, and
especially, the written codes of Paul), as we break into the new
life which Christ gives. At the same time, Torah is not rendered
useless. God sent his son 'in order that the just requirement of
the law might be fulfilled in us' (8:4). We are no longer to
measure our righteousness by our success in obeying Torah.
But Torah still sets before us the ideal of love which we are
now to find in a different way, through the power of the Spirit
within us. It is not abolished; it is transcended and completed
by the person of Christ.

Matthew himself did not seem to draw the conclusion that
Torah was abolished. Perhaps he was one of those who wished
it to be retained in the early Church. But he agrees absolutely
with Paul that Torah cannot ever be properly obeyed without
the power of grace, union with the person of Christ who is the
fulfilment of Torah. It is right to remember, as we read the
sermon on the mount, that the one who speaks is not a giver
of external laws. He is one who will bring us into the blessings
of the Kingdom by placing his own risen life within us. It was
a conclusion established only after much argument, but seeming
inevitable with hindsight, that the early, predominantly Gentile, Church would come to feel that Torah itself was no longer
binding on the community of the new life.

It is still sometimes hard for us to see clearly that Christian
morality and practice must be founded, not on written laws

and traditions, but on living union with the person of Christ,
who calls us to see and do new things in his name. It is sometimes fear that binds us to the past. It is often love that leads
us into the future. It is always wisdom that teaches how the
past is to be at once fulfilled and transcended in a new future.
The sermon on the mount is itself the supreme example of how
this can be achieved. We follow it best when we seek to do the
same in our own very different contexts, seeking always to live
in Christ, to be 'rooted and built up in him' (Colossians 2:7),
not making of his words a written law, but seeing them as
evocations of the power and freedom of love.

Questions

1   Is it true that 'we are no longer to find the answer to moral
problems by looking in a book'? Using Matthew 5:19, Acts 15
and Romans 10, reflect upon how the Bible must still be used
as an authority in making moral decisions, even when it does
not give straightforward 'answers' to our moral problems.
2   'We stand under judgement and must live by grace.' Using
the Beatitudes, call to mind the many ways in which the
supreme moral demands of Christ are broken in our own lives.
Then use Matthew 11:28–30 as a prayer, relying on God's
promise of forgiveness.
3   Are there matters in the life of my Church when it must
break away from old written codes to find the new life of the
Spirit? Or where I must accept sincere differences of opinion
and outlook, held together in love?

8

Peace

'Blessed are the peacemakers, for they shall be called sons of God.' (Matthew 5:9)

In Matthew's presentation of the sermon on the mount, Jesus has set out the nature of true happiness. He has shown how the world makes happiness hard to achieve. He has shown how selfish desire must be replaced by the self-transcending love that Torah enjoins, if happiness is to be found. He has told his Jewish hearers that they must keep Torah, with a greater sincerity and inwardness than the groups of Pharisees who were opposing his teaching.

He next proceeds to set out, in a number of memorable sayings, just how Torah should be interpreted by his disciples. These sayings are often known as the Six Great Antitheses. Each one starts with the phrase 'You have heard' – that is the thesis. Then Jesus says 'But I say to you' – and that is the antithesis.

It has seemed to some that Jesus is here contradicting Torah, setting it aside and replacing it with a new teaching. But if the previous chapters were correct, this does not seem very likely. Jesus is keeping Torah, but showing how to interpret it. We Gentiles may not now keep Torah, but his interpretations will still reveal much of great importance to us, as we seek to know how to live, as disciples.

The first antithesis is: 'You have heard . . . "You shall not kill; and whoever kills shall be liable to judgement" . . . but I say to you that every one who is angry with his brother shall be liable to judgement.'

Jesus does not here contradict Torah at all. It is still true that you should not commit murder; that is, you should not kill an innocent person (that is what the commandment in Torah actually says, in Exodus 20:13). He seems to make it much more stringent. You should not even be angry. That certainly fits with the idea that your righteousness must exceed that of the scribes and Pharisees. Jesus is extending a commandment about external behaviour so that it also covers what we might call 'murder in the heart', the internal feelings which might lead to murder.

He takes this even further. For he says that anyone who insults another shall be liable to go before the council, the Jewish supreme court, or Sanhedrin; and anyone who says 'You fool!' shall be liable to the fire of Gehenna. Taken literally, he is saying that calling someone a fool is actually worse than murdering them (for it seems to merit a worse punishment).

This is an important clue to the fact that Jesus' statements in this sermon are not to be taken with stolid literalness. A few verses later the point becomes glaringly obvious. 'If your right eye causes you to sin, pluck it out and throw it away,' he says. And 'if your right hand causes you to sin, cut it off and throw it away' (5:29, 30). Now there are many peculiar varieties of Christian churches in the world. But as far as I know there is not among them a sect of one-eyed, single-handed true believers. No one has ever been tempted to take this text literally. Even Origen, who castrated himself on a rather similar principle, did not pull his eye out. In any case, if you want to be really literal about it, the text only refers to the right eye; so perhaps if the left eye causes sin, that is all right.

The attempt to take the text literally is very obviously absurd. Worse than that, it would miss the whole point. Jesus is not talking about the right eye, as opposed to the left. It would be the worst sort of legalism to think that. It would be precisely the sort of thing Jesus opposed above all else. He is not talking about physical actions at all – he is not seriously suggesting that we pull our eyes out or chop our hands off.

To see what he is saying, we need to realize that there is a very common style of Jewish teaching which was often used by rabbis. What it does is to use very exaggerated, hyperbolic statements – which are very memorable – to make a simple point. These sayings are rather like proverbs, like 'too many cooks spoil the broth', for instance. They are not to be taken literally, as if one could find an equation giving the ratio of cooks to the mass of accumulated broth for all kitchens. The English proverb means that using too many people for a job can lead to confusion. But no very precise and unambiguous interpretation can be provided, which will apply to all situations. Proverbs are essentially vague and suggestive. They may apply to many different types of situation, but they may also be counteracted by other proverbs, which point in quite a different direction (to take the example given, 'many hands make light work' would do precisely that). To take proverbs as absolute rules would be silly. But they can be useful reminders providing general advice for all sorts of cases.

The statement about pulling eyes out is rabbinic hyperbole – or, as we might say in English, proverbial. Jesus reminds us, in a very picturesque and memorable way, that false perception and wrongdoing are very serious. If persisted in, they will bring us to Gehenna, to destruction. The cause of false perception and evil must be eradicated. We must attack the root of illusion and selfish desire, if we are to be whole. That is the meaning of Jesus' words. If we interpret them as being about mutilating our bodies, we miss the spiritual meaning completely.

Thus we cannot take the first antithesis literally – as though it is wrong to call your brother a fool, but quite all right to call your sister an idiot! We must look for the underlying spiritual meaning. We might then say that anger felt in the heart is wrong. If one allows anger to express itself in abuse and insult, that is worse. And if one treats another person with contempt, that threatens to destroy one's own soul.

It is important to stress that this is not an infallible interpretation, by any means. The whole point of proverbial discourse is that it must remain suggestive, not clear. Each person can then reflect upon it for themselves, and draw a personal meaning from it, which applies to their own situation. Part of the point of the gospel record of Jesus' teaching is that it should be used for personal meditation. It may convey something different to different people at different times. It is always capable of bringing new insights. The most useful procedure is often for a group of people to discuss their different insights, and so increase their common awareness of the depth of the teaching. What I am trying to bring out is the general character of the teaching. I am absolutely not claiming to give one 'true' interpretation.

What can we say about this first antithesis, then? First, that it does not contradict Torah, with all its rather complex rules about unlawful killing. Second, it tells us that we are not only to consider the external act of killing. Inner attitudes like anger also contradict God's law; they cut one off from God. Third, the rule is extended to cover, not just unlawful killing, but all cases of hating and abusing others and holding them in contempt. Fourth, it is not merely negative, saying 'do not', as though it would be all right if one did nothing at all. For it goes on to say, if you remember that your brother has anything against you, go and be reconciled. We have to do something positive, to heal broken human relationships and misunderstandings. In other words, Torah does not just say that you should not kill people. It says that you must build up positive friendly relations with people. Instead of hating, insulting and despising them, even in your heart, you must love, respect and honour them, extending the hand of friendship as widely as you can. As the example of Jesus shows, this is to include outcasts and sinners as well as those whom one naturally likes.

Jesus thus teaches that the commands of Torah are meant to relate us rightly to God and, at the same time, to bring us to personal wholeness and realization. They are concerned with inner attitudes, and they cover the whole of our thoughts and feelings towards others. They require positive action, and they require us to exclude no one from our God-given task of being reconcilers and peacemakers among our fellow human beings. In this way Jesus shows how the seemingly simple commandment, 'You shall not kill', which seems so easy to keep for most of us, in fact places before us an ideal which covers all our thoughts and feelings, which we can never completely attain.

This antithesis relates to the seventh beatitude, 'Blessed are the peacemakers'. For the ideal attitude which is placed before us by Jesus is that of being bringers of reconciliation and peace.

The beginning of real peacemaking is to honour every other human person, in every thought and feeling. The way to begin to do that is to see them justly, as God sees them. And the way to do that is to see in them the face of Christ. When we see Christ in all people, and all people in Christ, then we can start to be true disciples. Christian discipleship is to grow into that ideal. Once again, keeping Torah is not a matter of obeying a set of external rules and regulations. It is founded on the perception of an ideal, and the love for it. The Christian life is not legalistic or infantile obedience; it is a continual seeking to grow towards the ideal of Christ.

It can now be clearly seen why it would be a dreadful misunderstanding to interpret these sayings of Jesus literally. The strictly literal interpretation would be much too narrow. Whereas Jesus is teaching about inner attitudes of respect for all people, the literalist view would merely rule out calling people fools or insulting them. The literal interpretation is too easy; it lets us off the hook too much. Moreover, it would be an example of just the sort of thing Jesus always condemned – the legalistic observance of rules while missing their spiritual point. No set of rules can exhaust the attitude to which Jesus is drawing attention.

It follows that it may sometimes miss the spirit of the rule to insist on keeping it absolutely, or without exception. Consider, for instance, whether Jesus is really saying that it is wrong to be angry, in all circumstances. Some have interpreted it like that, but it is very difficult to do so. Jesus himself drove the money-changers out of the Temple at Jerusalem, and he spoke angrily to the Pharisees when he called them 'whited sepulchres and hypocrites'. Jesus was angry at sin, especially religious hypocrisy. And surely if one sees a child being tortured, it is right to be angry at its torturers? On a more mundane level, we all know that sometimes one has to be angry to get anything done. Is it not unrealistic to think that Jesus is ruling out anger altogether?

Some early Christians clearly felt this difficulty, for in some early manuscripts of Matthew's Gospel, the words 'whoever is angry *without a cause*' are inserted. These are not the earliest manuscripts, so it seems that this is a case of an early interpreter trying to make explicit his view that Jesus was not ruling out anger on all occasions. There are some times when anger is permissible. He does not say what these are, so it is left up to us to decide when there is just cause for anger. This is in line with the commandment forbidding killing in Torah, which allows killing for a just cause – in war or for punishment, for example.

It seems that there may be just causes for anger, then. The hard problem is how to respect people while being angry with them. But the problem is not insuperable. One can be, and often should be, angry with one's children, but one can and should continue to love them. Where anger is meant to lead to the ultimate restoration of a guilty wrongdoer, and where it does not preclude such restoration, it is permissible. Indeed, it is probably true that a failure to be angry at actions which cause harm is itself a sin, and a disservice to the wrongdoer, who may not see the gravity of his offence. In fact, in this very antithesis, Jesus implies that it is just for an offender to be imprisoned until he has paid the last penny. So he is not opposing punishment or judgement as such.

As at least some early editors of this Gospel saw, Jesus' words, which may seem to forbid anger entirely, do not do so when taken in their context. That shows the danger of seeking to absolutize these sayings of Jesus. There may always be exceptions to them. They are not absolute rules. They are not really rules at all. What they do is place before us an ideal for our inner attitudes, which will determine the sort of person we are. We are not told exactly what to do, on all occasions. We are told what sort of person to become. When we have done so, then we can make our own moral decisions.

This, then, is our guide to interpreting the other antitheses. Jesus is not setting aside Torah, but deepening and broadening its interpretation. The fundamental stance he asks for is that we should see our lives not in terms of rules, but of vision; not in terms of principles, but of a new perspective on life; not in terms of obeying duties, but in terms of a continual drawing nearer to a supreme ideal. Jesus has become Torah for us, so that he is the ideal towards which we strive. For the Christian, that ideal is not some impersonal abstract construction. It is a living and definitively human person. He is the Teaching, the Word, the image of the invisible God (Colossians 1:15) in finite and personal form. The content of his teaching is himself, and we follow it best when we are united to him in love.

Questions

1 'Every one who is angry with his brother shall be liable to judgement.' How do I interpret that? To what actions and feelings in my own life does it apply?

2 What can we do to bring about a greater peace in our own hearts? In our local neighbourhood and workplace? And in the world at large?

3 'You shall not kill.' When is it permissible for a Christian to take life or to be angry with another? What can we do to increase our reverence for all life on this planet, and to stop taking life unnecessarily?

9

Purity of Heart

'Blessed are the pure in heart, for they shall see God.'
(Matthew 5:8)

The Christian religion can sometimes seem to be obsessed with sex. When people talk about Christian ethics, they often think only of such things as contraception, adultery, homosexuality and so on – as if these were the main topics of ethical debate for Christians. This most unfortunate impression is in fact quite false. What Christianity is concerned with, in ethics, is above all the dignity of the human person. It is concerned with learning how to honour personhood in others and in our hearts. This is as much, or more, a matter of helping people to grow and develop their creative potential than it is a matter of having a set of restrictive rules about sexual practices.

Nevertheless, sexuality is important. Humans are sexual beings, and their sexuality enters deeply into their self-understanding. As human beings can become perverse through selfish desire, so their sexuality can become perverse through lust. Lust is inordinate desire for the pleasure which comes through sexual stimulation. Such desire can lead to a lack of respect for personhood, in oneself and in others. When it does, it is wrong.

The Bible is never opposed to sexual enjoyment as such. The Song of Solomon celebrates the physical joys of marriage, and the Church has always condemned those who think that sexual enjoyment is wrong by its very nature. It is a God-given gift, and should be celebrated as such. It is wrong only when it is wrongly used; and that is, when it leads us to dishonour human personhood. The fundamental principle of the Christian attitude to sexuality can be summed up in this brief statement. It is what Jesus brings out in the second antithesis: 'You have heard that . . . you shall not commit adultery. But I say to you that every one who looks at a woman lustfully has already committed adultery with her in his heart.'

We can examine this teaching in the light of the points already established about the first antithesis. First, Torah is not set aside. Adultery is having sexual intercourse with someone else's wife. That remains forbidden. What underlies the rule is that human sexuality is an essential part of human nature. It cannot be split off and treated as a separate area of love, without involving other human feelings, attitudes and commitments. When you have intercourse, you give yourself to another person in the most intimate relationship possible to human beings. It is both a physical act and a deeply personal act. To split the physical from the personal, to say that you can have sex without personal involvement or commitment, is to misunderstand human nature completely. Sex should be the deepest expression of love, and love is a total commitment in trust to another person. When two people have made that commitment, it is always wrong for another person to seek to destroy it. That is why adultery is wrong. Jesus does not set that teaching aside.

Second, what he does is to stress that the commandment applies to inner attitudes, not just outward actions. Just as anger is wrong, so regarding another's wife as an object of sexual enjoyment, even in the heart, is wrong. It regards the woman as simply an object of desire, without a commitment of love, and it lessens respect for the life-long relationship of mutual trust and love which characterizes Jewish and Christian marriage.

Third, he extends the commandment over the whole range of human thought and feeling. It is not just wrong to look at a married woman lustfully. It is also wrong to regard anyone else simply as a means to one's own enjoyment, as an object to be used and not as a person, worthy of respect and deep personal relationship. Thus the commandment applies to pornography, intentional perversion and any other human feeling or thought which devalues human personhood.

Fourth, this is not to be taken as an absolute rule, stating that one should never look at a woman lustfully. This may sound strange, until one considers that a strict, literal interpretation of Jesus' words would rule out looking even at one's own wife lustfully, or with desire. That would make many wives justly annoyed, and it is obviously not what any Jew could have meant. This point should hardly need making, if Jesus' words had not been misinterpreted so often by people who are afraid of sex in any form. We need to stress that sexual desire is natural and good, when it is properly orientated.

In our society, many regard sex as a casual means of pleasure. In prostitution and 'one-night stands', one does not consider a sexual partner as a person at all, but as an object for gratification. However, every act we do affects our own humanity. We may think such activity leaves the personal aspect of self untouched, but it does not. Subtly and gradually, it leads us to regard other persons merely as objects. Even worse, it leads us to think of the other sex as a means to obtaining our desires. It corrodes the quality of our personal relationships. Instead of seeing others as persons for whom Christ died, as images and children of God, we see them as physical pleasure-objects. Machines would do as well, if they were constructed cleverly enough. So our vision is fundamentally corrupted. That soon begins to show in thoughts and actions which treat some human beings as less than persons. It is no accident that sexual perversion very often accompanies tyrannical and inhuman political regimes. As Jesus said, 'If your eye is not sound, your whole body will be full of darkness' (6:23).

How can we avoid this corruption, by which others become either slaves to our wishes or tyrants of our fantasies? Only by placing sexual practice firmly within a fully personal commitment of love. Sex is humanized when it expresses a true caring for another person as such. Such caring requires a long-term commitment to loyalty, whatever befalls. It requires faithfulness, in the sense that one promises to help and care for another for better or worse. It requires an acceptance of responsibility for the care of children who may naturally result from sexual intercourse. And it requires a readiness to use this secure relationship as a base for extending friendship and hospitality to those around. All these things require a commitment for life, a commitment which nothing can sever. And that, of course, is the basis of marriage. When Christians say that sex should occur only within marriage, they mean that sexuality only finds its true meaning within a total commitment of love and faithfulness, wherein there can be absolute security.

It should be remembered that marriage in Jesus' time was not like it is today in Europe. Most marriages were arranged by families, and perhaps the bride and groom would not see each other until the wedding night. Marriage was not based on physical attraction, on 'falling in love'. Indeed, falling in love, that invention of women's magazines, is a very bad basis for a life-long commitment. It is intense, ephemeral and variable. It is essential, if marriage is to survive, that we should think of love as a commitment of the will, to care and cherish, not as a convulsion of the heart, which may fade, leaving nothing behind.

The breakdown of marriage is always a profoundly disturbing event, as the sad distresses of the children of broken marriages show. A marriage should be a secure base in which children can be brought up and cared for, a centre for an expanding set of personal relationships, with an unshakable inner core of fidelity. That is why Jesus condemns the thoughts and feelings which may undermine such a relationship of mutual trust for the sake of a little physical pleasure.

This antithesis relates to the sixth beatitude, 'Blessed are the pure in heart'. To be pure in heart is to see others, not as desirable bodies with souls peripherally attached; but to see others as embodied souls, their bodies as sacraments, expressions of their souls. Only when we learn to see others thus, as images of God calling for our reverence and love, will we be able to see God himself, the self of all things, to whom supreme reverence, love and worship, are due. With this in mind, Jesus gives us his promise: 'Blessed are the pure in heart, for they shall see God.'

The third antithesis is really a second part to this one. Jesus reminds his hearers of the teaching in Torah that any man who divorces his wife should give her a written statement of divorce

(Deuteronomy 24:1). But he adds that every one who divorces his wife (except for unchastity) makes her an adulteress (5:32).

We need to interpret this teaching in the same way as the others. Jesus does not rescind the legal permission to obtain divorce. Torah remains in force. But he states very forcibly that divorce is wrong, that it undermines that relationship of trust and loyalty which is at the basis of positive and secure human relationships, and which makes the rearing of children in love and safety possible. Again, it would miss the point of the teaching to take it legalistically or as an absolute rule. Taken literally, it is just not true that a woman becomes guilty of adultery, and therefore liable to be stoned to death (Deuteronomy 22:22), if her husband divorces her. This is another example of memorable hyperbole.

'Adultery', in its literal sense, is having sexual intercourse with someone else's spouse. Jesus breaks through to a deeper level of meaning; he takes adultery to be the destruction or impairment of a marriage. In this wider sense, you commit adultery whenever you do anything to harm another's marriage. You even commit adultery when you harm your own marriage, by neglect, jealousy or irritability. It is in this sense that a man who divorces an innocent woman is guilty of 'making her commit adultery' – making her the destroyer of the marriage. That is because the man will divorce her because he is displeased with her in some way, and thus implicitly puts the blame on her for the breakdown of the marriage. Thus Jesus teaches that divorce is always a failing and an imperfection; it is a sin in the strict New Testament sense that it is a missing of the mark of human perfection.

In the culture of the day, it was only possible for men to divorce women. The precise wording of these two antitheses makes it sound as if they are addressed only to men, who can look at women lustfully or divorce them. But to interpret them in this strict and restrictive way would again be to miss the whole point of Jesus' teaching. He addresses women as well as men, and what he says applies to all the sexual attitudes of human persons as such. In its own context, it is reasonable to see Jesus' teaching as a condemnation of the practice by which men could divorce their wives for almost any reason, and leave them without means of support or social position. There is little doubt that Jesus opposes such a practice, which treats women as possessions, to be disposed of when one is tired of them. But the whole nature of Jesus' teaching, which is about all one's inner attitudes to the building up or destroying of human relationships, leads us to broaden the interpretation to cover any form of marital breakdown.

To take this teaching legalistically would be to make it only apply to men wanting to divorce their wives or to marry divorced women. In fact, however, it applies to men and women alike, within marriage as well as outside it. For a good marriage is not just a question of continuing to live together. It is a matter of continuing respect and care. It is, quite frankly, hard work. It is easy to point the finger at adulterers and accuse them of sin. But it is harder to realize that we may be committing 'adultery' within our own marriage, destroying it by lack of love as well as by infidelity in the heart.

Jesus points, then, to the inner attitudes of fidelity and trust which should permeate all human relationships. He demands of us that we work positively and continually to build them up and cherish them. Whatever our views or the views of our own Church may be about the extremely complex questions of divorce and remarriage, it would certainly miss the whole spirit of Jesus' teaching to think that he was here merely condemning divorce. Of course, it is clear that he regards divorce as a missing of the mark of good human relationships that God has set before us. But his teaching is much wider than a concern with social arrangements of marriage and divorce. It is about the inner attitudes which build up or destroy those relationships of trust and loyalty which find their supreme expression in marriage.

The teaching should not, therefore, be taken legalistically, in a strict and literal application to all conceivable circumstances. Nor should it be taken as an absolute rule, so that one is bound to live with a marriage partner for ever, whatever happens. No major Christian Church has accepted such a hard teaching, though churches have rather different ways of coping with clear marital breakdown. Matthew recognizes the point by the insertion of the phrase 'except for unchastity' (5:32).

Whatever exactly unchastity is – the Greek word is *porneia*, and there is much scholarly dispute about what it means – Jesus apparently here allows divorce for certain reasons. The three Synoptic Gospels all report this saying of Jesus about divorce, but the other Gospels do not mention this phrase. For that reason, some scholars think that Matthew inserted it because he found the words of Jesus too difficult to accept. This is not the place to enter into scholarly debate on this topic; the object of our meditation is Jesus as Matthew sees and reports him. We must therefore assume that Matthew took himself to be reporting the intention of Jesus, whether or not these are the actual words. We therefore have to say that Jesus, at least as far as Matthew is concerned, is not forbidding divorce in all circumstances, any more than he forbade anger in all circumstances. In the sermon on the mount, if a relationship has been irretrievably broken by one's partner, the recognition of that breakdown by a formal act of divorce is not condemned by Jesus.

We have already noted that the precise words of Jesus need not be taken as binding on a Christian Church. So this point does not settle the extremely complex and disputed question of divorce and remarriage today. The Churches must proceed to consider prayerfully and come to their own decisions, just as the early Church did in the case of keeping the Torah. But we must say, of Matthew's depiction of Jesus, that he opposes divorce very strongly, while permitting it for just cause (where the exact nature of that cause is left unspecified). Again, then, we do not have an absolute prohibition here. So it is natural to say, as we did with the first antithesis, that Jesus is not giving a rule; he is, rather, placing before us an ideal of absolute trust and fidelity. That is the model for Christian marriage, and it is an image of the absolute commitment of love that God makes to us, and of our union with Christ, that nothing in heaven or earth can destroy.

Questions

1   In my sexual life, have I failed to respect the personhood of another as fully as I might? Have I used another solely as a

means to my pleasure; or have I neglected to think of their pleasure? How can I learn to see them more humanly?

2 Do I show fidelity, loyalty and trust in my personal relationships with others? Do I use my friendships as a base for extending love and hospitality to others? Does my family life look out towards others, or is it a cosy inward-looking hideaway?

3 Whatever one's views about divorce, marital breakdown is a tragic and destructive force. What can we do to support its victims, and to strengthen marital ties, without falling into the trap of judging others?

10

The Teacher

'You have heard . . . "You shall not swear falsely" . . . But I say to you, Do not swear at all.' (Matthew 5:33–34)

Quakers are among the very few Christian bodies which have taken the fourth antithesis at its face value. One of the features which first distinguished them was that they refused to swear on the Bible in courts of law. They are, of course, quite right in pointing out the irony of swearing on oath on a holy book which tells them forthrightly not to swear on oath. In fact, Jesus goes much further, and adds: 'Let what you say be simply "yes" or "no"; anything more than this comes from the evil one.' For Catholic and Anglican priests, the position is even worse, for all of them have to swear allegiance to their bishop, despite the words of Jesus, 'Do not swear at all'.

Of course, this will not seem so strange if one accepts the way I have interpreted the first three antitheses. I have held that they cannot be taken literally. This may have seemed slightly shocking. But it turns out that the vast majority of Christians throughout history actually agree. For most Christians think that to keep the words of Jesus about swearing on oath literally would be to miss the point of his teaching. One can fully keep the spirit and truth of his teaching, while contradicting the words he actually says.

The importance of this point can scarcely be overestimated, when thinking about how Christians today should make moral decisions. It needs to be clearly borne in mind, whenever one is faced with some apparently clear words of Scripture on a moral issue, and wonders how binding they are. For the vast majority of Christians, and for all those in the oldest traditions, this antithesis forces a clear answer upon us – the *words* themselves are not necessarily binding. We have to reassess for our own age and situation what the underlying teaching is. That will often be a matter of disputed interpretation. It seems to me that this, at least, is indisputable. If Christians could learn to take this to heart and live with it, it might make a very big difference to our view of moral decision-making, and to moral differences and divisions within and between the Churches.

The fourth antithesis can now be interpreted in a way consistent with the interpretation given of the first three. Jesus in no way rescinds Torah. If you make an oath, you must keep it. What he does is to say that we should be so honest and reliable in our dealings that we never need to swear an oath. Our word alone must be our bond. What is required is absolute honesty and truthfulness. Again, Jesus points to the inner attitude of truthfulness, which is to be extended throughout the whole range of our thoughts and feelings, and to include a positive striving for truth. Integrity is part of Christian discipleship, and faith can never be opposed to the most resolute honesty with oneself and others.

To take the statement literally would be to miss these points almost entirely. For then it would only apply to swearing on oath – a very restricted subject for Jesus to be concerned about. Most people would think that it may be permissible to swear on oath, where that is required by authority, and where it does not compromise honesty. Jesus is not giving a precise command, to be obeyed to the letter. He is showing what sort of persons we must be, if we are to enter into the Kingdom – persons of absolute truthfulness. Again we see clearly that to take Christian morality in terms of rules, old or new, is to miss the heart of it. It is growing into an ideal, growing into the mind of Christ, that living, personal reality upon which we shape our lives; which in fact shapes itself in us, as we allow it to do so. Christian morality is not obedience to rules. It is the transforming love of a person.

The fifth antithesis can be interpreted in a similar way. Jesus quotes the law, repeated three times in Torah, 'an eye for an eye and a tooth for a tooth' (Deuteronomy 19:21). This law was never, so far as we know, taken literally. It pointed to a general principle that the punishment should fit the crime. Far from denying this principle, Jesus reiterates it by saying 'the measure you give will be the measure you get' (7:2). He clearly teaches that there is a cosmic law of moral equivalence. God's law remains that people will be treated in the way they treat others, and that is exactly the principle of 'an eye for an eye'.

Nevertheless, some people quote the sentence, 'If any one strikes you on the right cheek, turn to him the other also' (5:39), as though it was the sole element of Jesus' teaching. It is taken as recommending total pacifism, and it gives rise to Nietzsche's famous criticism that Christianity is a religion for masochists which encourages weakness and invites others to walk all over you.

Those who take such an interpretation usually have not seen how very extreme a literal view of this antithesis would be. For Jesus also says 'Do not resist one who is evil' (5:39). If that was literally true, no Christian could be a police officer, a judge or even a parent. We would have to stand by and watch while evil people murdered, raped and plundered what they wanted. In the same section, we find the statement, 'Give to him who begs from you, and do not refuse him who would borrow from you' (5:42). As soon as anyone hears about this, they will quickly ask to borrow all our belongings, and very soon we will have nothing left. Jesus seems to be teaching total non-resistance to evil and complete poverty. Nietzsche infamously took this interpretation: 'Being a soldier, being a judge, being a patriot; defending oneself; preserving one's honour; desiring to seek one's advantage; being *proud* . . . The practice of every hour, every instinct, every valuation which leads to *action* is today anti-Christian' (*The Anti-Christ*, page 38). Nietzsche, of course, is opposed to such a view. But is his interpretation of the sermon even half-way plausible?

It is possible to take a literal interpretation of the sermon on the mount. But if you do, you will not be able to take part in most of the activities of a normal social life. Anyone who is committed to not resisting evil people will have to put up with a soaring crime rate, with exploitation and oppression, and with being a virtual slave without any property. There will be no church building – for one must give it away or allow it to be taken away without resisting. There will be no houses, for the same reason. There will not even be a communal dwelling-house, unless some kind person donates one. Even then, it would only be ours until someone, less kind, came along and took it away. In other words, we would be wholly dependent on the kindness of others. We would be parasites, relying on others for whatever protection we enjoy. Or, more likely, we would very soon become wholly extinct!

This sort of interpretation is only possible for a 'gathered community', set apart from the world, living in complete poverty, strict chastity and obedience to whatever law is imposed upon them. Has the sermon then nothing to say to the rest of us? Has it nothing to say about our human responsibility to build up societies of social justice? Does it really rule out our defending innocent victims from evil? Or even defending our own families and those who depend upon us and giving them security and justice? If justice requires the exercise of force to restrain the unjust, are we for ever condemned by Jesus to endure injustice?

If that were so, the sermon might well be thought to be irresponsible and even immoral. It would also then notably contradict the whole nature of Torah, which was designed to set out rules to govern a just society, and set out principles governing the justified use of force to restrain evil. It would negate the idea of human responsibility to build a just society, within which goodness can be encouraged. And it would constitute a decisive denial of the whole character of Jewish teaching, which is concerned with human good and flourishing in the material world that God has made and whose fulfilment he desires.

This can hardly be Matthew's understanding of the sermon, since he prefaces it with the statement that Jesus has not come to contradict Torah. The idea of a small gathered community, existing by the permission of its powerful neighbours, is as far as possible from the Jewish dream of the nation of Israel, set among others as a world power. To the extent that one takes Jesus as a genuine inheritor and fulfiller of the ideals of Judaism, therefore, the literal interpretation of the sermon cannot be accepted.

Another possible path, taken by Albert Schweitzer, is to say that the sermon does propose a very extreme and unworldly ethic. But that is because the disciples expected the world to end at any moment. There was therefore no point in owning property or being concerned about the future. There simply was no future to speak of. Christians were to centre their thoughts on the other world, and give up this one entirely. That makes the sermon completely useless for us. It was based on a false belief, and has nothing relevant to say to us now.

This seems a desperate course to take with a text which has been a moral inspiration to millions of people. We do not know that all Christians thought the world would quickly end – the second letter of Peter, which speaks forcibly of the end of all things, is careful to note that a thousand years to us is only one day in the sight of God (2 Peter 3:8). And Paul reprimands those who gave up work because they thought the world would end soon (2 Thessalonians 3:11). While there was a fairly commonplace expectation that the world might soon come to an end, among Jews and cultivated Romans alike, Christians also had a command to preach the gospel to all nations. They saw that God's time-scale might be very different from theirs. In any case, Matthew presents the sermon as a commentary on Torah, not as a millenarian tract. So perhaps we should not regard the sermon as based on a false belief, and as being morally irrelevant, unless no other and better interpretation is available.

There are other interpretations which have been widely accepted in Christian history. One, more prevalent in Catholic traditions, is to divide Christian morality into counsels and precepts. The precepts tell all Christians what they must do, as a minimum code. The Ten Commandments are usually quoted here. But there are also counsels of perfection, which might not apply to all people, but only to those who 'would be perfect'. For those few who go beyond duty to pursue perfection, the counsels of the sermon apply. This was usually taken to apply to monks and nuns, who can separate themselves from the world and live lives of poverty, chastity and obedience. Such groups are parasitic on the Church, which acts as a normal worldly institution, owning property and defending it against those who would take it away. They follow a more perfect way, a way with greater dangers and greater rewards.

This is a much more attractive possibility, but it still has difficulties. Is the sermon irrelevant to most Christians? And how does one know whether one should pursue perfection or remain content with following the precepts of the faith? Can there really be two sorts of Christians, living on two levels? The Protestant Reformers insisted that all are 'called to be saints', which seems to break down any clear distinction between the 'religious' and other believers. Again, while monasticism is a genuine development in the Church in response to a sense of particular vocation, it is so contrary to the ethos of most Jewish teaching that it seems unlikely to have been what Jesus really had in mind.

It is apparent that the sermon is harder to interpret than one might think. One might have wished for a Saviour who would leave us with a few clear, hard and fast rules. One might have wished that he could also have told us about the theory of relativity and a few other general principles of physics and saved a lot of trouble later in history. It seems, however, that these were matters which God wished us to discover for ourselves, by the arduous but exciting process of reflection and discovery. This is as true in morals as it is in physics. We have to discover for ourselves the precise details of how to live the good life.

What Jesus seems to do is to put a series of questions against our alleged certainties, and to speak in such paradoxical yet piercing aphorisms that we are continually forced to rethink our position again and again. It is remarkable that Jesus, perhaps the greatest moral teacher of all time, never wrote a book. Of course, he already had enough rules – six hundred and thirteen of them. There was little call to issue more! But there may be a deeper meaning in Jesus' literary reticence. Being a moral teacher is not, after all, a matter of being able to write books. It may not be a matter of telling other people what to think at all. The true moral teacher is one who has the capacity to undermine restricting interpretations of old traditions; to put a question mark against unreflective certainties; to evoke from others new insights of their own and to bring them to a better understanding of themselves, their limitations and their potentialities. If that is so, the words of the sermon will be interpreted best when they are taken as disclosing the person who spoke them, and who waits to speak to us anew through them in fresh ways.

Questions

1   Is it possible to be absolutely honest at all times? What does being truthful mean in my daily life – in ordinary gossip, in discussing my colleagues or neighbours, or in my work?

2   'If any one strikes you on the right cheek, turn to him the other.' How should I interpret this teaching of Jesus? When I apply my interpretation to the other antitheses, how does it work out?

3   What makes a great moral teacher? Did Jesus teach any moral rules? In what way was he a moral teacher?

11

Mercy

'Blessed are the merciful, for they shall obtain mercy.'
(Matthew 5:7)

Three main interpretations of the sermon have been considered, the third of which – the distinction into precepts of
duty and counsels of perfection – seems to be the most positive
and helpful. But we have seen that it rasies difficulties about
the apparent discrimination between two classes of believers,
the 'really religious' who seek perfection, and 'the rest', who
seem relegated to second-class status.

In consequence of these difficulties, a Protestant version of
this interpretation grew up. There were not two sorts of disciples, pursuing different moral norms. Instead, every Christian
person has to pursue two different sets of moral norms in
different phases of his or her own life. One could follow the
counsels of the sermon in one's life of personal discipleship,
and yet follow a very different set of principles in social life,
as a judge, soldier or teacher. However, it is impossible to split
a human life into distinct pigeon-holes in this way. I am almost
always acting as a parent or child or member of a tennis-club
or whatever. There hardly seems any sphere of purely personal
morality to retreat to. This sort of view has perhaps been
responsible for the thought, fairly common in Protestant communities, that religion is a purely inward, personal affair, and
that it has nothing to do with social life and political decision-
making. Religion is concerned with the inner life. Of course,
that is quite true. One of the chief things that distinguishes a
religious morality is that it is concerned with what sort of person
you are, and not just with what you do.

But what you are does affect what you do. The inner life must be exressed in outward action. It is silly to say that I am very humble inside if I wear lavish clothes and have a large and luxurious car. It is like saying that Iam highly intelligent inside, even though I always say stupid things. True humility must show itself in action. Suppose, however, that I am the Prime Minister, and am required to entertain in some style and to ride in grand cars, as part of my job. Does that mean the Prime Minister cannot be humble? It's no use telling the Prime Minister she should be humble in the bath, or wherever it is that she is not being Prime Minister. It looks as though there are still some people to whom the sermon cannot apply.

So yet another interpretation emerged – that the sermon places before us a set of 'impossible obligations'. It tells us that we are commanded by God to be absolutely honest, open, humble, poor and charitable. Yet God places us in a world where we must deceive, conceal, insist upon our rights, protect property and fight in order to survive and protect those who depend upon us. So it is impossible for us to meet our obligations. What is the remedy? The only remedy is to rely solely upon grace, upon God's free forgiveness. In other words, we are given obligations we cannot keep; we are declared guilty for not keeping them; but then we are forgiven anyway. It does seem a most peculiar way of going on.

The view is not really as absurd as this makes it sound. There is a sense in which most people feel that they canot live up to their own ideals, but they need to be constantly reminded of these ideals. When they fail to live up to ideals, they need to know they are accepted and enabled to go on. But it is too paradoxical to put this by saying that you are guilty for things you cannot help. If that is what the sermon on the mount does to people, it is more likely to turn them into neurotic wrecks than anything else. To give someone a sense of permanent failure is psychologically disabling. Christianity is dreadfully misused when it does that to people. We may well think it wrong, then, to teach anything that might impart such a feeling, under the guise of a gospel.

In recent years there has been a reaction against moralistic interpretations of the sermon – interpretations which seem to impose a very rigorous set of duties on us, and make us feel guilty for not being able to fulfil them. The German theologian and New Testament scholar Joachim Jeremias has proposed that the sermon is not a moral tract at all. It is not meant to tell us what we ought to be doing. Rather, it simply describes what life in the Kingdom is like. It is Gospel and not Law. What it does is to draw a picture of the Kingdom of God, a Kingdom of love, peace and justice. Then it proclaims that Christ places us in the Kingdom by grace – not by our moral efforts. We will begin to live like that when we are filled with grace. That can begin today, in so far as we are reborn in Christ. What the sermon does is to proclaim the promises of God, describe the life of the Kingdom, and call for our repentance and faith in Christ, who gives the Kingdom freely to us.

This view still has a great emphasis on the free and gracious love of God. But it does not require any great feelings of guilt or of enormous moral burdens. It is pure proclamation of what God will do for us, if we let him. This is certainly an attractive and hopeful picture. The difficulty is that Matthew does, despite all Jeremias says, seem to be issuing moral rules. The antitheses have the form of commands – 'I say to you . . .' Moreover, they presuppose the existence of evil, otherwise there would be no evil to resist. So it does not really seem to be a picture of the Kingdom of perfect reconciliation. It is more like a commentary on how to apply Torah in a very complex and ambiguous world.

The fact that I have been able to give six quite different interpretations of these sayings, each of them held by an entirely reputable section of the Christian Church, shows how hard they are to interpret. Anyone who thinks that the teaching of Jesus on moral issues is clear and straightforward is simply ignoring Christian history and theology. The figure of Jesus does not stand as a perfectly clear authority which declares to us what we should do. It stands as a mysterious challenge to all our moral reflections. The challenge is always there, driving us to ask again whether we have really taken the measure of what is required of us. But what it drives us to do is to reflect further, to face up to the demands of God's love more clearly. It gives no predetermined answer. The ambiguities in Jesus' teaching will not go away. It looks very much as though they are intended to teach us something. And what they teach is that there is no escape from our individual responsibility to respond to God's love in our own unique way and situation.

My own interpretation of the sermon, which claims to be no more than a personal and partial perception of the riches it contains, is that in it Jesus places before all of us a set of ideals of character. These depict the sort of person who is the child of God, the member of the Kingdom. In this respect, Jeremias is right. These ideals are found portrayed in the character of Jesus himself, which must provide the main clue to interpreting his teaching.

An ideal is quite different from a duty. A duty is something you are obliged to do. Everyone has a right to expect you to do your duty. You are not praiseworthy if you do it, but you can be blamed if you fail to do it. An ideal, on the other hand, is not something you are strictly obliged to achieve. You may have the ideal of being a graceful swimmer. While it is right for you to try your best to achieve the ideal, no one will blame you if you do not succeed. In fact, it is positively praiseworthy to achieve a high ideal, and no one has a right to expect you to do so, or can blame you if you fail. Ideals are usually things people set themselves – to be courteous, or hardworking or studious. But the ideals which Jesus sets before us are the ideals which God has set into human nature itself. They are not optional. They are ideals for all human beings.

Is it not a soft option to replace duties by ideals, which no one will blame us for not achieving? The point is that we do have a duty to do our best to achieve the ideal. But no one knows exactly what our best is, so no one else can ever judge us for not living up to it. Each of us knows, individually, that the ideal stands before us, drawing us towards it. When we rightly see the Christian ideals in the person of Christ, we know without a doubt that we have much yet to do to come near them. This is not an easy moral option, for the ideal continually exerts its demands upon us. It sets no precise standard which others can accuse us of failing to meet. But it always asks more of us, as we respond to it in our own way. We have to try to achieve as much of the ideal as we can. So different people may achieve different sorts of ideal, in different forms and degrees. There is nothing wrong with that. This is, I think, the truth that the medieval distinction between precepts and counsels was expressing.

In the sermon Jesus *is* telling us how to live. He is presenting a set of ideals that each one of us must internalize in our own way. It is true that Matthew can seem to be a very rigorous moralist, asking us to obey God's will right down to the smallest dot and comma, with a greater degree of righteousness even than the most observant Pharisee. But it is precisely this hyperbole, this element of bold exaggeration, which gives us the clue to what he is really saying. We begin to see that we are to transcend law altogether, and break into the realm of Divine love, which Jesus opens up to us. He *is* Torah, and we obey Torah to the full when our wills are lost in his love.

If we apply this interpretation to the fifth antithesis, it does make coherent sense. When Jesus says 'Do not resist one who is evil', he is not giving a rule, telling us to allow evil to flourish unchecked. If this were true, we could not even resist evil by word or look or exhortation, which is ridiculous. Jesus takes the picture of a person who insists on his rights, on the exact punishment for every wrong. And he contrasts it with the picture of a person who always attempts to bring good out of an evil situation. This alternative picture is rather like the one that Socrates draws in *The Republic*, when he says that a good man will never cause harm. So, Jesus seems to imply, it is never enough to ask that a person should be harmed because they have harmed someone else. Certainly there must be punishments and deterrents; Torah is not rescinded. But we must always look to the good even of those who have done great evil.

It is not a Christian response to hit someone just because they have hit you, even where the law allows it. Licensing vengefulness does not make it good. We are not to oppose – that is, we are not to seek to annihilate or harm – even a person who is evil. We are to seek their good as well as we can. The possibilities of doing this may be very limited. We may be forced to kill someone to protect others. If someone runs amok with a machine-gun, perhaps all we can do is kill them. Even here, in the extreme case, our intention must be to prevent harm to others, and not to kill. And in many more ordinary cases, our treatment of an offender will be very much mitigated by our consideration, not only of the harm he has done, but of how he can be best helped to find a better life.

On this interpretation, what Jesus is saying is that retribution, though it has its proper place, is not enough. We must have in mind the reformation and restoration of the offender, whether he has offended against us or against the public order. In applying the law, the Christian should never do more harm than seems to be strictly necessary, and he should never give up the possibility of bringing the offender to a better state. This principle explains how it is that Jesus, as an upholder of Torah, could accept the justice of capital punishment for murder, while his teaching strongly suggests that such punishment should never be applied.

The precise formulation of the examples used in this antithesis depends upon local circumstances in Jesus' time of which we are not fully aware. Jeremias tells us that striking a person on the right cheek was an insult, and that Roman centurions could compel Jews to carry their packs for one mile. Jesus is suggesting, then, that we should not respond to insults with insults; that we should do more to help others – even members of an occupying military power – than they can strictly require of us.

To understand Jesus' teaching, we need to consider, not the precise actions he discusses, but the intentions which may lie behind them. Jesus is not suggesting that we should intend to let people walk all over us. There would be no value in such an intention. We must intend that the opponent is turned from evil in his heart. If turning the other cheek cannot accomplish this, if in fact it encourages the evil-doer to think he can get away with more, then it is useless. Once again, the application of the saying requires wisdom, to know when and how it applies. What it enjoins is mercy – the consideration of what will turn the heart and mind of the evil-doer, rather than simply of what legal punishments are available. It may be that the enduring of insults will remove bitterness and anger. If so, it is always to be pursued rather than observance of the strict letter of the law. But if it has no such effect, or if it even breeds contempt, then one must take necessary restraining action.

The mainstream Churches have always accepted this, in the doctrine that there is such a thing as a justified war of self-defence. Certainly, if Jesus was not abandoning Torah, he would have to accept the rules of warfare which figure prominently in it. It is highly unlikely that Matthew regarded Jesus as a pacifist, or as someone who opposed retribution as such. Such practices as capital punishment and even a war of conquest are firmly embodied in Torah. As we have seen, on Matthew's reading, Jesus accepted Torah. So he must have accepted the justifiability of such practices. What he asks of us is that we do not rest content with the justifiability of a practice. We should always seek to maximize the welfare even of aggressors and offenders, not always insisting upon our legal rights. Jesus' teaching does not take away the need for great wisdom in dealing with practical affairs. It points to the attitudes which must underlie the application of such practical wisdom.

Jesus' words in this antithesis apply primarily to the inner attitude of willing harm to none, if it is avoidable. This can be seen as a comment on the fifth beatitude, 'Blessed are the merciful, for they shall obtain mercy'. What Jesus tells us is that if we would wish to be treated with mercy by God, then we should be merciful to others. It is not that we should simply let them off everything. But we should not insist on the strict retribution that we might rightfully exact from them.

Jesus typically extends the idea of mercy even further, to cover all attitudes of aiming at the good of others to a greater degree than is strictly obligatory. When he says that we should not refuse 'him who would borrow from you', he is not advocating gross profligacy, or a practice of giving everything away to the first person who asks. He is advocating openhearted giving, and a concern for the needs of the poor. As to how this should be done, or to what extent, the sermon is silent. Its whole point is to challenge us, in prayer and private reflection, to come to our own judgement of what more we can and should be doing in these respects. It will apply very differently to a soldier on active service, to the trustee of a major charity or to a worker in a wealthy European country. It will have some application to each case, but what that should be is left to the judgement and sensitivity of the individual.

In this way, paradoxically, the most conservative reading of the sermon is the most radical in its conclusions. Taking Matthew at his word, we are bound to see Jesus as upholding Torah. We are therefore bound to see the words of these antitheses as proverbial discourse, as not literally applicable. That forces us to deny that Jesus' ethical pronouncements have final and definitive authority for us, just as they stand. We are compelled to say this, however, not out of some perverse radical impulse, but precisely on the authority of Jesus himself. Our ethical task as disciples of Christ is not the task of putting into practice a set of clear commandments. It is the harder one of discerning the Spirit, seeing how to move towards the ideals which Christ places always ahead of us, drawing us closer to himself. This is not a soft option. It places before us the unyielding demand and the true grandeur of the ideal of Christ. It forcibly reminds us that it is always easier to keep definite rules than to be cast upon the sea of love and personal responsibility. It gives us responsibility, but insists that true responsibility is always a response to a greater and wider love.

Questions

1 Does Christian morality fill me with a sense of guilt? Or does it help me to accuse others of guilt? Can seeing the sermon on the mount as the good news of eternal life help me to overcome this guilt and free me for a less critical attitude to myself and others?

2 What is the difference between ideals and duties? Attitudes and rules? Virtues and obligations? Does Christ teach us ideals, attitudes and virtues, and leave us (or the Church of which we are part) to devise particular moral rules?

3 'Do not resist one who is evil.' How can we apply this to our modern society? What is the right Christian attitude to criminal offenders and to those who oppress others? How far can mercy modify retributive justice?

12

Love of Enemies

'Love your enemies and pray for those who persecute you.'
(Matthew 5:44)

The sermon on the mount does not add an additional list of duties to the moral life. It places before us the ideal of a wholehearted concern for the well-being of others, a life lived out of care for the flourishing of all God's creatures. Thus, in the sixth and final antithesis, Jesus stresses that we should not confine our concern to our friends and families. Torah never says 'Hate your enemy'. But no doubt much popular teaching had stressed concern for fellow Jews more than concern for Gentiles. The scandal Jesus caused by eating with Gentiles showed how religious piety could come to exclude others, and give rise to misunderstanding and hatred.

Jesus' teaching is clear: we must love all people, even those who oppose our most cherished ideals. We should care for their good and seek to understand what they desire and pursue. Often we will still have to oppose others; they will remain our enemies. Yet we should not cease to care for their good, and we should never regard them as less than human.

There are some strains even within Christian thought, unfortunately, which can easily lead to hatred, misunderstanding and the demonization of opponents. We find some of them within the New Testament itself. If all Jews are referred to as 'scribes and Pharisees' and described as whited sepulchres, for instance, this can give rise to unthinking hatred of Jews. And when John tells us to hate the world, this may easily become hatred of non-Christians, or of Christians of some other sect than our own.

It has to be confessed that there is something in the nature of Christianity which has led to hatred and violence against others. It is no accident that persecution and repression have been such obvious features of Christian history. I suppose one chief reason for this is the idea that Christians have the absolute truth, which is divinely revealed. So anyone who hears and re-jects it must be evil; they must be rejecting God himself. Thus rejection of one's own beliefs becomes blasphemy. Disbelief must therefore be punished or even exterminated. Unbelievers must be devil-possessed; therefore one can treat them as devils, as sub-human, no longer deserving of respect. All this is quite opposed to the teaching of Jesus, who asked from the cross that those who had condemned and mocked him might be forgiven (Luke 23:24).

There are a few passages in the New Testament which can unfortunately be interpreted to give a view very unlike that of Jesus. This would of course be a misinterpretation, but it can easily arise when the passages are taken out of context. Strange as it may seem, one of them comes in the first letter of John, who speaks more than any other writer of the love of God. The writer captures the spirit of Jesus exactly when he says 'He who says he is in the light and hates his brother is in the darkness still' (1 John 2:9). Yet some readers may seize on the fact that it is one's *brother* that one is to love. Now we would naturally think that everyone is my brother; so this must include love of enemies too. But this fact may be missed by a careless reader.

Things may be made worse, when John goes on to say: 'Do not love the world or the things in the world' (2:15). What he means is that we should not love the pleasures which come by selfish greed, passion and envy. But he writes further: 'Many anti-Christs have come' (2:18). He then refers to people who have left the Christian fellowship. He calls them liars, and says that a liar is 'he who denies that Jesus is the Christ' (2:22). Such a person is an enemy of Christ and of God the Father.

What he says makes perfectly good sense, in its original context. But the words have given rise to many regrettable beliefs. Even though it is a distortion, one can see how we might move from saying that 'the world' is opposed to God, to saying that all non-Christians are opposed to God. Then Jews, Muslims and humanists all become enemies of Christ. Very soon, our love is confined to the brothers within the Church, and everyone outside it becomes an enemy, to be avoided as much as possible.

The second letter to the Christians at Corinth contains a passage which has given rise to similar misunderstandings. 'Do not be mismated with unbelievers,' says the writer (6:14). 'What fellowship has light with darkness?' He then quotes the prophet Isaiah (52:11), saying: 'Come out from them, and be separate from them, says the Lord' (6:17). Again, there is an appropriate way of understanding this passage, but it has given rise to terrible misunderstandings. The prophet Isaiah is speaking to people who are escaping from exile in Babylon. He tells them to keep themselves ritually clean when they carry the equipment for the new Temple to Jerusalem. The New Testament writer uses this passage because he is writing to a small community of disciples in a city in the late Roman Empire. It is full of all the vices of decadent imperialism – superstition, sexual licence, dishonesty and greed. So he reminds them of the need for true holiness; a 'keeping apart' from all the vices of the city, and a rejection of those who claim to undermine the gospel of freedom he had preached. But does this mean that Christians must separate themselves from the world altogether, and have no relations with unbelievers? Does it mean that all unbelievers really are enemies of God?

That simply cannot be true. Jesus ate with publicans and sinners. So the meaning is not that Christians cannot mix with unbelievers. It is that Christians must be careful to maintain the purity of their commitment to the ideals of Christ. We must be 'in the world but not of the world', which seems an admirable way of putting it. Similarly, there is no comparison between those who clearly saw the meaning of Jesus' Messiahship and then rejected it to return to the Corinthian fleshpots, and those today who honestly cannot believe there is a God or who are offended by the intolerance and prudishness of many Christians, and find greater freedom outside the Church. They are wrong, no doubt. But they have not rejected a clear vision of God in favour of selfish greed.

It is only an unreflective reading of such passages, together with a failure to relate them to the gospel teaching of Jesus, which can lead to intolerance and exclusiveness. But we must be aware of the terrible ambiguity of the Christian faith, when it gets into the hands of people like us. Like any system of religious belief, it can lead to great harm as well as great good. The best way to counteract that harm is to become aware of it, and not conceal it or pretend it is not there.

Even if we decided that the world outside the Church was full of enemies of Christ, that would not mean that we must hate them, or that we should ignore them and leave them to their own devices. Against all such views Jesus clearly says 'Love your enemies'. If someone hears and rejects your beliefs, you must still love them and care for their good. But may it be for their good to burn them, and maybe save their souls? Perhaps so, if it did save their souls. But there is no reason at all to think that it does.

The real problem goes deeper. Does the particular sect to which you belong really possess the whole of Divine truth? And are people who cannot agree with the way you put things really disagreeing with God? Have you put things so clearly and indisputably that when they reject you they are rejecting God himself? There is a danger here that we might confuse ourselves with God. This is the most subtle form of spiritual pride, and perhaps the most dangerous sort of all. It is subtle, because we might sincerely believe we are completely humble. Are we not doing the will of God? Declaring the truths of God? Simply being his humble and devoted servants? So it may seem. Yet others might see that we are in fact equating our words with the words of God, and thereby claiming for them an absolute authority. Is that not the epitome of pride, to put oneself in the place of God?

So we see ourselves as divine, and our opponents naturally have to become demonic, the forces of evil, trying to destroy our own precarious citadel of truth. The stage is set for a battle to the death, in which God is on our side, and the other side is wholly evil. We do not need to understand it – indeed, it is better not to dabble too much in evil, lest it influence us. So ignorance becomes virtue, hatred becomes love, and paranoia becomes the highest wisdom. We are surrounded by enemies; we see ourseves as the only remaining defenders of the faith. Even our friends are liable to betray us, as we discover more and more minute differences between them and us. We make ourselves martyrs for the cause of truth, deserted and betrayed by all, but valiant to the end, the only true church is a world at the very gates of Hell. If that point comes, we should know that we are probably suffering from a dangerous mental illness.

It is vital to recognize that religion can do this to us. In the sermon on the mount, Jesus tries to point this out. He says 'Beware of false prophets' (7:15). Now you may think that the false prophets are those who disagree with you. But even though Jesus does show us the supreme truth about God, our grasp of that truth may very well be incomplete and inadequate. So we cannot call someone a false prophet just bcause they do not see things in the same way that we do. In fact, Jesus gives quite a different way of telling a true prophet from a false one. He says 'You will know them by their fruits'. What are the good fruits for which we are to look? They are classically presented in Galatians 5:22 – love, joy, peace, patience, gentleness, goodness, fidelity, humility and temperance. By contrast, the evil fruits are hatred, gloom, argument, impatience, rudeness, hypocrisy, fickleness, pride and intemperance.

The test question is: do religious teachers show these fruits in their own lives? And do their teachings produce such fruits in the lives of their followers? If the fruits of your teaching are ignorance, hatred and fear you begin to sound like a false prophet. It does seem as though the teaching that my group has the fullness of Divine truth, that rejection of it is rejection of God is a false teaching, according to the very criterion Jesus proposes to us. For it very easily leads to arrogance (if I have the full truth, I do not need anyone else to tell me anything) and pride (for I tend to confuse rejection of me with rejection of God, and you cannot get much prouder than that).

There is no reason why any Christian group should think it possesses the whole truth about God. The Torah explicitly says 'The secret things belong to the Lord our God, but the things that are revealed belong to us and to our children' (Deuteronomy 29:29). Many secret things about God and his purposes remain unknown to us. The main Christian traditions about God agree that he remains incomprehensible and beyond human understanding. It is out of the question, then, to have the *whole* truth about God. Nor is it the case that *everything* any group believes about God at a given time is bound to be true. The apostles, or some of them, believed God would bring the world to an end very soon, but he did not. And one may confidently assert that every Church errs on some matter at any given time.

This does not affect the claim of the Roman Catholic Church to possess a teaching authority which is, on rather rare occasions, protected from error in its official pronouncements. That is a very restricted claim which allows that many opinions held by the highest authorities and popes about God, but not thus formally defined, have been mistaken. Nor can one hold that no other group possesses any truth about God. Christians are committed to asserting that a great deal that Jews say about God is correct. Nor can we plausibly claim that our group can have nothing to learn from any other group. We will not know unless we find out what they think. And they may have seen things we have missed or unduly neglected in our own way of putting things.

Of course orthodox Christians believe that Jesus is the Word of God made flesh; he *is* the truth. But our grasp of that truth is always partial and defective in some ways. It is always in need of completion and enlargement, and this may come from unexpected quarters. So we cannot say that our presentation of the truth is adequate. It follows that rejection of our teaching is not equivalent to rejection of God's truth itself. In fact, much atheism can be seen as a protest against the immoral and irrational way in which the Christian faith has sometimes been presented. We perhaps bear the responsibility for principled atheism as much as many of our opponents. We must be slow to judge the hearts of men; and Jesus is quite clear about that too.

There is accordingly no excuse for failing to love our enemies. And we must see clearly what love requires. It is not just a negative thing. It requires of us that we do something positive. A minimum requirement of loving someone is that we understand how they see things, what they want and what they hope for. We do not have to agree with them, by any means. But we cannot seriously claim to love them if we are not even interested in what they think and why they think it, in their experiences and perspectives on the world. So we cannot be uninterested in, or afraid of, the beliefs and values of our 'enemies' and opponents. We have a duty to understand them, and the reasons for them, as well as we can. There is no place for caricature and ridicule in Christian love. There is a lesson here for the modern Church, as we meet those of other faiths and beliefs. What we have to proclaim to them is a liberating message of love and freedom, not a repressive huddle of fearful and spiteful minds, nor an arrogant assumption of superiority.

Love of enemies is indeed hard to put into practice. But it is the summation of the virtues that Jesus places before us, as implications of the revealed will of God. The person without anger, without lust, without infidelity, without dishonesty, without vengefulness, without hatred – that is the person to whom the Kingdom belongs. In that person the Kingdom already lives and grows. There the mind of Christ is formed, and those who live as disciples of Christ become the body of Christ in the world. They are those of whom Jesus speaks when he says 'Theirs is the Kingdom of heaven'.

Questions

1   Who are our real enemies? How can we understand them better? How can we care for their good, while opposing them?
2   Is there anything in my religious faith or practice which leads, however unthinkingly, to hatred, dislike or caricaturing of others? Where might it lead me to intolerance or exclusiveness? Do I really know enough about the views I reject as wrong or evil? Am I really sure that the way I understand things embodies the absolute truth?
3   Using the list of the fruits of the Spirit (Galatians 5:22), consider how far our religious beliefs lead them to grow in our lives and in the lives of those around us; and how far some of those beliefs may stunt their growth.

13

The Anti-Christ

'Judge not, that you be not judged.' (Matthew 7:1)

Not everyone has seen the sermon on the mount as the highest moral teaching. There are those who think that it is actually stupid and immoral. It is worth spending a little time considering what is said by one of the most influential of these critics, to discover what justice there is in what he has to say, and what insights one might find even in his very negative response.

Friedrich Nietzsche said of himself: 'I am the *anti-Christ*' (*Ecce Homo* 3:2). It is therefore not surprising that he has mounted one of the most sustained and vehement attacks upon the teaching of the sermon on the mount in the history of literature. Much in his little book, *The Anti-Christ*, seems to be filled with hatred; much is based on various speculative and now mostly rejected accounts of the presumed teaching of Jesus and the early growth of the Church; and much is morally repellent. The tragic thing is that this marvellous literary stylist was, in part, saying things that are actually in the sermon itself. Jesus was as critical of religion as Nietzsche ever was, though of course Jesus hardly rejected it wholesale. What might Christ think of the latest prophet and self-styled opponent to the death, Zarathustra?

First one must mark the shrill and arrogant note which Nietzsche strikes, as he begins his work. 'We are the Hyperboreans', he says, the people who have discovered happiness, who are brave and unsparing of themselves and others, who refuse to resign themselves to the world of weaklings, the lazy herd.

There is immediately an irony in striking this firm note. For it is not long before he accuses the hated Christians of arrogance in thinking that they shall judge the world (page 45), and of moral perversion in rejecting 'the world' as rotten and corrupt (page 46). More like these Christians than he thinks, he stands in judgement on the world of weaklings, and waits for others to catch up with his insights and his revaluation of all values. He, like them, discards the world of petty affairs and social convention, and advances towards a realm of freedom, life and happiness.

But there is a difference. He is contemptuous of those who remain among the weak. He finds pity to be a denial of life. And he commits himself to the will to power, the overcoming of resistance, a continual war in which the weak and ill-constituted shall perish. His is a philosophy of strength. One of his gravest charges against the Christians is that they promote active sympathy for the weak (page 2) and advocate equality before God. On the contrary, he cries, you must embrace strength, power, victory; revel in your power and strive for magnanimity, the benevolent display of power and wealth and the celebration of your superiority to other men.

A reasonably unbiased spectator might think that Jesus has already revalued all values more thoroughly than Nietzsche will ever do. For the Zarathustran prophet retains in place and unimpaired that most basic and destructive value of all things that common men love – the will to power by any means and for any end one chooses. He is contemptuous of the weak, but he needs the weak to make power possible. If one really wished to turn human values upside down, one would say instead, as Jesus did, that true strength is to be found in weakness, true power in loving service.

But Nietzsche will not have that. He takes the secret longings of the crowd and proclaims them as virtues for the cruel and the strong, in whom the weak must live vicariously. When Christians claim to judge the world, they refer to the judgement of love upon selfishness and greed. When Nietzsche judges the world, he refers to the judgement of the boot ground into the head. No wonder he hates these Christians, who preach love and pity.

But why does he hate them so? It is because he blames the gospel for reducing man to a herd animal. It takes the side of everything weak, base, ill-constituted. It is anti-life, and it revels in misery. It is the mewling protest of the weak against the strong. It is the morality of *ressentiment*, of revenge, a revenge deferred, it is true, to the after-life, but desired none the less. It is wholly opposed to the noble morality of those 'strong emancipated spirits' who rightly claim to govern mankind by their strength and will to life. When it conquered the noble might of Rome, it undermined the Empire, and reduced Western man to decadence.

This is a strange judgement on a religion which produced the Crusades, wars and trials of strength in sickening abundance. But he is right – these wars are anti-Christian, however much they use the name of Christ. Should one then reject the Christian gospel because it condemns war and the struggle for power? War is the greatest destroyer of human life there is. It takes human bodies; it batters, tortures and mangles them, blows them to pieces or sends them back twisted beyond recognition. Is that to be called life? And is the spiritual overthrow of one of the greatest military tyrannies in the world, the imperialistic conqueror, ancient Rome, to be accounted failure?

What is corrupt in Christianity is not the pity which brought gladiatorial combat to an end, but the imperium of Rome which crept into the faith and lived there a new secret life. Jesus Christ is the Lord of Life. He came to give life more abundant, and to give the joy of sins forgiven and the conquest of death. How can that be seen as anti-life?

Ah, but are the life-affirming instincts not blunted and repressed? Are we not told to be meek, humble, non-resistant to any evil, accepting all things? And does that not mean giving up the struggle and conflict which affirms and celebrates power? Here is the old misinterpretation of the sermon, tired and implausible even in the hands of a master. According to it, Christians are to be miserable, life-denying, cowed and persecuted members of what he calls at one point a 'Buddhistic peace movement'. Where, in all this, is the power – yes, power indeed – of the Spirit, Divine power poured out on the followers of Jesus, sending them throughout the known world to face torture, imprisonment and death?

Above all, where is the Jewish heritage which is present and emphasized in Matthew more than in any other Gospel? The joyous affirmation of life under one's own fig tree, with a glass of wine and a thriving family; the preparedness to defend the promised country; the joy of the presence of the Spirit of God; the pride of an honest day's work well done and deserving of its due reward – all these things are ignored by the searching eye of Nietzsche.

What he misses is a central and vital part of Christian morality, the element of paradox which is never far away. We must be meek, yes; not thinking that we possess any virtues or capacities by our own creation alone, to be utilized as we wish. But this does not mean being always apologetic and self-deprecating. The gifts of God are to be used rightly, proper responsibility exercised and authority claimed where it is due.

Nietzsche can hardly fail to see this point. But, having complained that Christians are too meek and mild, and thus anti-life, he then complains when they begin to make claims to rule the world and to have the wisdom of God. Suddenly they become too arrogant and proud. But what he sees as a contradiction – the meek claiming Divine authority – is in fact precisely the revaluing of the idea of authority which he should himself be seeking. It is an authority which expresses, not the proud self-will of a victorious people, but the demands of God which restrain all political power and place it firmly under moral control.

Naturally the exercise of such spiritual authority can go wrong. Anything human can go wrong. Nevertheless, if one gives supreme honour and authority to someone because of their moral and spiritual office, there is more chance of abuses being rectified in due course than if one gives such honour to whomsoever is strong enough to hold it, and for just as long.

Nietzsche sees the Christian morality of humility, chastity, poverty and holiness as a morality of the weak, seeking revenge against the strong. A strange revenge indeed, which seeks only to love its enemies, and counsels that only those who forgive will be forgiven! Why does he see this as a morality of revenge? Why does he think of Paul as the 'genius of hatred'? (page 42).

What he proposes is that Jesus was a sort of Galilean Buddhist, teaching peace, love and non-resistance – strange that he exempts Jesus from his condemnation of Christianity, as though even the anti-Christ is compelled to acknowledge some spark of moral grandeur there, however misguided it might be. But Paul turned the group of 'little abortions of bigots and liars' who were the first disciples, into a pack of vengeful world-haters. He did this by introducing the ideas of punishment, guilt, judgement, sin and immortality – apparently all of them foreign to the thought of Jesus – into the new religion. Paul did not believe this himself, one understands. But 'what he himself did not believe was believed by the idiots among whom he cast his teaching' (page 42).

So the first Christians do not actually have to take revenge on their enemies. They leave it to God, who will damn them to Hell. What the Christians do is worse than overt physical vengeance; it is a corruption of morality at its root. Instead of the joy of intellect and the senses, honours, life, beauty and bravery, they praise the 'virtues' of the weakling under-class – hatred of the body, of sex, of reality itself. In their morality, there is from the first 'a certain sense of cruelty towards oneself and others . . . hatred of those who think differently; the will to persecute' (page 21). Hostility to the masters of the world tries to encompass everything in its own nihilism, its fundamental 'cowardliness and weariness of soul' (page 18), that instinctive hatred for actuality which is 'the only driving element' in Christian faith (page 39).

Perhaps we should be grateful that Nietzsche exempts Jesus from most of his moral strictures. Unfortunately, we cannot accept this dispensation, since it is precisely this Jesus who, as recorded in the Gospels, speaks so much of judgement and sin, and who defends the resurrection of the dead against the Sadducees. One cannot lay these things at Paul's door; they must be traced to Jesus himself. It is Jesus who must be taken as the genius of hatred.

But what an extraordinary judgement on the one who taught that anyone who calls his brother a fool is in danger of judgement; that one must love even one's enemies; and who offered forgiveness to all who came to him. The judgement is made by one who finds in the Gospels only a 'strange and sick world . . . in which the refuse of society, neurosis and "childlike" idiocy seem to make a rendezvous' (page 31). The hatred seems to be in Nietzsche, not in Jesus.

In point of fact, both Jesus and Nietzsche expose the self-deceptions of religion quite ruthlessly. Nietzsche points out the secret vanity which can afflict believers, when they claim to speak with the voice of God. Jesus does the same, when he rails at the Pharisees for claiming the chief seats in the synagogue and praying in public so that they may be admired for their piety. Nietzsche points out how belief in immortality can lead to neglect of the importance of life in this world. Jesus does the same, when he stresses that our eternal reward will depend on how we behave in this world. Nietzsche points out how the ideas of punishment and Divine judgement can be used to terrify and condemn our enemies. Jesus says 'Judge not', and preaches the good news of God's free and full forgiveness of sin.

Perhaps it is the very ideas of sin and judgement that Nietzsche dislikes. That shows he has not felt the force of the reality of evil, not in others, but in himself. Indeed his own list of 'noble virtues' resonates with the danger of evil. He values bravery, beauty, life and luxury. Yes; but he also values the will to power, the 'grand passion' which gives to the strong man 'the courage for unholy means' (page 54) and which rejoices in the thought of a Borgia as pope (page 61). Convictions are prisons, he says; they should be used as means to the strong, life-affirming, brave and adventurous passions. Before long, Germany was to find such values ruthlessly embraced by Adolf Hitler. Lacking the subtlety and irony of the prophet, he demonstrated what the will to power without 'moralic acid' could really be like. Faced with that spectacle, would one still wish to say that Christianity is the greatest corrupter of the human soul?

Can anyone view the Holocaust, and not believe in sin? Can anyone think of it, and not cry out for judgement? Can anyone remember it, and not pray that a God of love will restore life to those whose lives were so cruelly taken? Can any Christian contemplate it and not plead for forgiveness for the weakness and lack of understanding which helped it to occur, and which still disfigure our own grasp of faith? If Christianity is to blame, it is because it had not the courage to protest enough at the corruption of its own values by the ethic of the will to power. It is because it had not thought through the truth that its God is a Jew, who called his own people to be true to their tradition until the heavens fall.

Where Nietzsche's case is unassailable is where the Church has not been true to itself, where it has not faced up honestly to the dangers of hatred, judgement and spiritual pride which Jesus pointed out at the beginning of its life. Sometimes the Church has seemed to condemn joy, sexuality, love of beauty, freedom of intellectual pursuit and self-affirmation. It has called for an infantile dependence on authority and been afraid of the fearless search for scientific truth. Even so, it is absurd to say that Christians hate the body and political powers as such, together with life and health and joy.

Nietzsche saw that Christians stand squarely in the Jewish tradition – which he put with typical charity to both faiths by describing them as 'little superlatives of Jews, ripe for every kind of madhouse' (page 44). Their faith is therefore centred squarely on this world, the good creation of which they are stewards. Their God even took flesh upon himself, making the body holy for ever. He dwells in 'the beauty of holiness' and is a God of truth, in whose presence is endless joy. Moreover, he does not offer escape from life – that is more typical of the Buddhists of whom Nietzsche speaks less disparagingly – but requires that life in all its material details should become a sacrament of his presence. Christ offers health, life, joy and love – that is what salvation is. And he offers it now, although indeed its fullness is yet to come, when the Kingdom which is already present in Jesus is made manifest without ambiguity.

When Nietzsche looks at the sermon on the mount, he sees only negatives – a world-denying faith for the weak and envious, the depressed cowards who cannot face reality without illusions. It can only be seen thus by an almost heroic determination not to see it in its context. It does not deny the world; it calls the disciples of Christ to be a light for the world, to be perfect, to fulfil the potentiality which God has brought to be. It is not for the weak; only the very strong can voluntarily endure loss with joy. It is not for the envious; it is for those who do not care for wealth and possessions, but who give more than they are asked to give. It is not for the miserable or misanthropic; its keynote is happiness and it calls for unrestricted love.

But it may be that the Beatitudes, with their stress on the poor, on mourners, the meek, the hungry and the persecuted, do seem to be addressed to the weak. What have they to say to the strong, the healthy and successful? Is there anything here about the positive goals of life and the positive worth of human life? There is, though it is more something that is presupposed to the whole background of the sermon than explicitly brought out in the text. In the remainder of this study, I shall seek to elucidate these features, which set the sermon firmly in a general context of Christian ethics.

Questions

1 Is there any justice in Nietzsche's claim that Christianity is anti-life? That it is a morality for masochists? Are there elements in our own faith which might give cause for such accusations? How may we guard against them?

2 In what ways might pride, vanity and vengefulness enter into our faith? Have we rooted them out as completely as we can?

3 What has the Christian faith to say, positively, about the good things of life – about art, sexuality, intellectual freedom, courage and proper self-love?

14

Perfection

'You, therefore, must be perfect, as your heavenly Father is perfect.' (Matthew 5:48)

With this sentence, Matthew represents Jesus as summing up the commentary on Torah which he has just given. It is an echo of the statement in Torah itself (Leviticus 19:2), 'You shall be holy, for I the Lord your God am holy'. The Hebrew word, 'holy', *qadosh*, means 'set apart'; in the context of faith, it means set apart or devoted to God. But it soon came to have strong moral overtones of the purity and perfection which belong to God. The word 'perfect' is a good translation, since it brings out the distinction of God from everything imperfect and his superiority in value to all created things.

Up to this point, I have been following the text of the sermon quite closely. I now want to probe some underlying issues which are implicit in the moral teaching of Jesus. He has taken the authority of Torah for granted, and given it an interpretation which is both deeply orthodox and surprisingly radical. He has assumed that God is a real and living reality, and that the Kingdom is truly at hand, that it is even among his hearers already. But we live in a very different age, when God is no longer taken for granted, and when we can find it hard to see the relation between God and morality. We often find it even harder to see how morality can ever be a matter of obedience to a revealed 'law'. We cannot put aside the question of what the basis for morality is, and of how God relates to it.

So what I want to do now is to look at the question of the basis for morality in general and how Jesus' proclamation of the imminence of the Kingdom of heaven makes a difference to it. Since I will be moving into an area of fundamental moral thought, the discussion may seem a little abstract at times. It will not do much harm to skip over any parts which seem to be unduly boring. The reason I have included them is that these questions do have to be addressed by people who are seriously concerned with questions of the nature and justification of Christian ethics. The answers to them do make a difference to what we might go on to say about particular moral issues. But not everyone need take an interest in these more abstract questions. In that case, I hope that the key parts of the following discussions can still be taken as a meditation on what is meant by the 'perfection' of God our heavenly Father; and on how we might try to be perfect as he is.

This might seem to be an absolutely impossible demand. How can anyone be perfect? Does it mean that we must never make a slip or error of any kind? That we must be beyond reproach at all times? Who could live up to that? God is perfect because he is omniscient and omnipotent. He knows everything and can do anything. How could we be perfect in that way except by being God?

So it can easily seem that this command is either asking for the impossible, or that it is demanding a degree of moral purity which is quite beyond us. Then we might be tempted to discard it as impossibly idealistic. That would be a mistake. A better interpretation, much more profound and evocative, is suggested by the Greek word for 'perfect' which is used in the text. The word is *teleios*; and it means 'fulfilling one's end or purpose', 'achieving one's goal'. If we take the word in that sense, then we can say that, just as God fulfils his purpose simply by being himself, so we are to fulfil our purpose by fully realizing the goal of our existence.

This needs spelling out further. A purpose is a state at which one aims, something one tries to achieve. It is a state we want to be in, and are prepared to make some effort to achieve, if necessary. We all have purposes of many kinds. We might want to achieve a good income, or security for our family, or a very good stamp collection, or a high degree of skill at playing the guitar. All these are quite acceptable purposes, and we might spend a lot of time achieving them.

Purposes very often lie in the future. They can be things we have not yet got, but would like to get and think we can get. But purposes do not have to lie in the future. It might be our purpose just to go on with some activity we are at present engaged in. So a mountaineer may want to get to the top of a mountain. But his purpose is usually, if you examine it closely, simply to climb difficult slopes. If he just wanted to get to the top, he could take a helicopter. What he wants is to climb it himself. And then what matters is the skill, the risk and the effort itself. Our purpose might be to use certain skills we have. It might be to realize these skills as fully as we can, just for their own sake. We can see here how the idea of purpose can be connected with realizing our nature, with expressing the sorts of abilities we have been born with. We are born with skills and abilities, with a certain character. Our purpose might be to realize that character as well and as fully as we can.

So it is sensible to say that our purpose might be just to be what we are – to realize the natures we have, as fully as we can. Of course, to achieve such a purpose, we first have to discover what we really are, and then we have to know how to realize what we are, our natures and capacities, as fully as we can. In the end, this is the highest sort of purpose there can be.

The whole idea of purpose only makes sense if we think some things or states are worthwhile just for their own sake. Human beings often have great trouble in discovering what such states are. We often seek money or fame or status, only to discover the hard way that when they are achieved, they are not as worthwhile or as satisfying as we thought they would be. To seek for a really worthwhile purpose is to seek for something which is worth having just for its own sake, and not for any other reason. If we ever discover such a state, then the best purpose of all would be just to continue in that state. We could call this a state which realizes supreme intrinsic value. It is supreme because it is more desirable than anything else. It is intrinsic, because it is desirable just for its own sake, not as a means to anything else. We would wish such a state to continue for ever, if it could.

Some people cannot even imagine such a state. They are

always discontented, and would always be wanting to move on to something else, always seeking change and new experiences, without finding anything truly satisfying. Of course, a supremely desirable state does not have to be a static changeless state. Maybe it has to include change and variety. But this would not be just a sort of constant restlessness. It would be a state of continual satisfaction in each changing moment. It might be like listening to a great piece of music, where there is lots of change but a continued enjoyment, so that at each moment we are satisfied, not discontented. This intrinsic value would be a dynamic activity, always offering new experiences and offering supreme enjoyment as a whole and in each part.

What has all this got to do with religion? An important part of the religious quest is the search for something of supreme intrinsic value. We may not know, when we begin, whether there is such a value, or what it would be like. We may be wrong about it, and find that we imagine something that will be boring when we achieve it. Many people's idea of heaven does sound rather boring, unless you like playing harps or talking to angels. Probably we can only imagine this supreme value as a sort of expansion of what we enjoy at the moment. The reality might be very different, but we might not be able to understand it or see its value just now. That is no doubt why there are lots of different ideas of heaven.

The great religious teachers tell us that there is such a supreme value, something absolutely desirable just for its own sake. They usually talk about it in pictures and parables, so that we can understand it in terms nearer to our own experience. Jesus talks about it by talking about the Kingdom of God – a phrase which means the reign of God over the whole of our lives. The supreme value is God himself, and we find our supreme value by knowing and being united to God. When God reigns over our lives, his supreme value becomes something of which we are constantly conscious. It is not at all like some distant monarch sending down his laws, which we have to obey. It is the actual presence of a being of supreme value which we can know and love. The presence of God is what gives our lives supreme value.

It is important, then, to try to discover what the perfection of God consists in. When we say that God is good, we do not just mean that he happens to do good things. We mean that he is in himself the supreme standard of perfection. If we can discover this, we will know the ideal goal of the Christian life, the reality which we are to imitate in ourselves. Of course we do not have to do this in an abstract way. For we can know, quite simply and directly, that Jesus Christ shows what God is, that he who sees Christ has seen the Father (John 14:9). That is why the Christian life can be rightly spoken of as the imitation of Christ, who shows in a human life the unlimited perfection of God.

Since we are to imitate Christ, who bears within himself the fullness of Divine perfection, it follows that we will realize our purpose, our proper and full perfection, by following him. While we can do this very adequately simply by meditating on the person of Jesus Christ, it is often helpful to consider the perfection of God in a more systematic way. That will mean starting with a consideration of what our basic moral values really are, and then going on to see how they are both fulfilled and transformed in God. In this way, we may obtain a firmer and more ordered grasp of the full perfection towards which Jesus calls us as he speaks. But it is a good start to see that the gospel does not call us to deny human life. It calls us to seek its proper perfection. That is to be found, not by inventing some ideal of our own to pursue as we wish, but by coming to know and feel within ourselves the presence of God, which brings us to perfection by uniting us with the One who is the origin and fulfilment of supreme perfection.

Questions

1　What things are worth doing just for their own sake? Does my faith help me to achieve these things? Does it affect the way I think of them?

2　What is human perfection? Taking one of the Gospels, note down all the skills and abilities shown by Jesus. Consider how this gives us a picture of a perfect human life; and how I can imitate it in my own life.

3　In what ways does the gospel show us how to fulfil human

life and bring it to its greatest possible expression? What is my
picture of the Kingdom of God, in which such perfect lives
might be lived?

15

The Objectivity of Value

'Our Father who art in heaven, hallowed be thy name.'
(Matthew 6:9)

If we are to understand what it is that we must imitate, we must understand the nature of the supreme value of God. To put it rather dryly, the perfection, the goodness of God, consists in this: that he possesses the greatest possible degree of the greatest possible number of the most desirable of all intrinsic values. That probably seems a very abstract way of putting it. It is a rather formal way of saying that 'God is the greatest'! It can be helpful to spell these things out in formal ways, just to be sure that they make good sense. But of course the Bible puts it more poetically: 'Let them praise the name of the Lord, for his name alone is exalted; his glory is above earth and heaven' (Psalm 148:13).

When Jesus speaks of God, he is speaking of that being of unsurpassable glory. When we sit down to think about it we realize that such a God must possess all the values that he can. It may be impossible for us, with our limited imaginations, to know what many of these values really are, or what they are like. That is what we mean when we say that God in himself is incomprehensible. He is beyond anything we can imagine. But we can at least say that some values are 'basic', and God must possess those. If people value anything at all, they are committed to valuing these basic values. These are values if anything is; and everybody who thinks about it must accept them as such. They are necessary and universal values.

That may seem a large claim to make. Many people think that values are subjective, that they are matters of purely personal opinion. What's good for me might not be good for you. What's right for me might be wrong for you. And what's wrong for me might be right for you. So, such people might say, there's no reasoning about our values. Everybody likes different things, and it's useless to look for any common standard. It's even worse to look for some sort of 'objective value'. That would just be the attempt to impose our own values on others, and it is silly to try to do that.

That opinion might at first seem quite convincing, when we see all the different things people want. But if we look more closely, we may find that there are some necessary and universal values after all. We do not have to go around making a fairly arbitrary list of the things we desire, and trying to see whether everyone else desires them as well. We have to analyse the idea of value to see what is necessarily involved in the very idea itself. Once we have seen what a value is, we may see that there is a rather small list of values which must be accepted as values, if anything at all is accepted as a value. Then, whatever other values God possesses, he must possess these values to the greatest possible degree, if he is the supreme value of all.

If we can understand these values, we will understand a little of what it is for God to be good, to be supremely perfect. So what is a value? It is a state which could be rationally chosen by a free conscious agent. When I say 'This is of value', or 'This is valuable', I mean that I would choose it if I was free to do so, and if nothing else overruled my choice. Value is connected to choice. And choice is connected to freedom and knowledge. I can choose something only if I know what it is, and if I am free to do so.

So, if we accept anything as a value at all, we must accept that freedom, which gives the ability to choose any values, and knowledge, which gives us awareness of the range of possible choices, are values. These, then, are *basic* values – values which must be accepted by anyone who understands what a value is, and who values anything at all. Whatever you desire, you must accept that it is good to know where it exists and how to get it; and it is good to be free to get it.

Rationality is a value, too. For we need reason to be able to choose efficiently, to see how to get what we want, and to work out what it is we really do want. But why would we choose anything at all? The obvious answer is, because we want it; because it satisfies our desires; because, in the most general terms, it makes us happy. Whenever anybody asks 'Why did you choose that?', it is always a good answer to say 'Because it makes me happy'. There is hardly any better answer that could be given. If what we choose has no other disadvantages – if it does not make other people miserable, or make me miserable tomorrow, or in some way impair my future prospects for happiness – then happiness is always a good reason for choosing something. I am not saying that it is the only good reason, and I am not saying that everybody knows what happiness really is. I am merely saying that happiness is another basic value. We might not want to say that people should only aim at happiness. But we will have to admit that it always makes sense to aim at happiness. We will have to admit that happiness is a basic value, which we must accept if we accept any values at all. It is hard to see how anyone could really disagree with this – though of course people will argue endlessly about what happiness really is. That is a topic we will have to come back to.

So far we have four basic values – freedom, knowledge, rationality and happiness. But there is a fifth value which must be quickly added to the list. For we do not live isolated on a desert island. We need other people if we are to have any chance of getting the things we want, most of the time. We cannot be really free to choose a certain sort of action unless other people help to make that freedom possible. I cannot be free to play the violin in a symphony orchestra unless lots of other people agree to play the other instruments. I cannot be free to go on holiday unless someone provides some transport. We all depend on the help of others in innumerable ways, if freedom is to have any meaning at all.

In the same way, I can hardly have any knowledge at all unless someone teaches me, and unless I learn many things from others. I am hardly likely to develop my rational capacities unless others help me to do so. And there is not much happiness that I can obtain which does not involve other people. Most sorts of happiness come from joint activities with others, or sometimes from simply being with them and sharing experiences with them. It is quite plain that as human beings, we are unlikely to realize any of our basic values without the help of others. So we have to add to our list a fifth value, that of co-operation, without which none of the others will be possible.

This completes the list of basic values. These are not all the values there are, by any means. But these values are basic, in that anyone who values anything is bound to value these things, if they think about it. If we think anything at all is a value, is good, we must believe that freedom, knowledge, rationality, happiness and co-operation are good. In one sense, this conclusion is trivial or obvious. So it should be. Because if the argument is right, these values will have to be agreed to by everybody. They will have to seem fairly obvious. If they produced any surprises, something would be wrong.

However, the strength of the conclusion should not be minimized. What it means is that values are not purely subjective preferences after all. It means that people cannot choose absolutely different and conflicting values. We do not have to rely on looking for coincidences before we can say that people share their basic values. These basic values flow from the very idea of what a value is. In any possible world, anywhere in the galaxy or even outside of it, in heaven or on earth, the co-operative pursuit of freely chosen rational purposes is good. That means it is objectively right to pursue this aim. Even more clearly, it is objectively wrong to frustrate such an aim or to contradict these basic goods. So it is objectively wrong to cause or increase pain, ignorance, slavery, foolishness and enmity. Here we have a truly objective basis for human morality. It does not depend upon any religious or factual beliefs about God or nature. It means that basic values are autonomous (they do not derive from some factual or religious beliefs) and objective (they do not depend on the fact that some people happen to like them).

Moreover, it should be stressed that these are not just values some people agree about. If these are values for any free rational agent, just because and in so far as they are free rational agents, then they are values for all free rational agents. So we have to say that these are good things for any rational being to aim at; and this is so, whether we *want* other people to aim at such things or not. In other words, they are not just values for me and my friends. I have to accept that it is good for any being to have freedom, knowledge, wisdom, happiness and the disposition to co-operate with others. That is a firm and unshakable foundation for morality.

If God is the supremely valuable being, he will be good in many ways that we cannot even imagine, in glory and beauty and majesty and holiness. But he will at least possess these five basic values in the highest degree. It is no accident that in fact these are precisely five of the most important traditional attributes of God that are present in the Christian tradition and in the Bible. When Jesus speaks of the perfection of God, he is speaking of the fact that God realizes supremely all these basic values. When we say that God is good, we mean that he is desirable above all things, for himself alone. And when Jesus speaks of the Kingdom, or the rule of God over us, he is speaking of how our lives are to be transfigured by this supremely good being. For in Christ God wills to draw us into his own life, and give us some share in his own perfection.

I have said that morality is in one way autonomous, that it does not depend wholly on some command of God. All the same, the existence of God makes a tremendous difference to morality. We can rightly say that in the light of God's existence, morality is completely transformed. For the moral life becomes the attempt to revere and love the absolute value of God's own being, and to reflect it in our own lives. We are to be mirrors for God's perfection. Our aim is not so much to become good, as to reflect goodness as clearly as we can.

Christian morality cannot after all be autonomous, if we mean that we must achieve goodness by our own efforts, in whatever way we choose. Rather, Christian morality should always be *responsive*. We look to the supreme goodness of God, and seek to let it be reflected in ourselves. To be perfect as God is perfect, means to let the reflection of his glory grow in us. The Christian life is not simply one of pursuing a set of basic values for ourselves. It is one of looking towards the perfection of God, and letting that vision transform our lives.

In that way the name, the inner nature, of God is hallowed, as our finite perfection becomes a mirror of his infinity.

Questions

1   Are there some basic objective values? What simple moral rules might one get from them?

2   Consider the perfection of God, his possession of all basic values to the highest possible degree. Consider how prayer and worship is the contemplation of God's perfection; and spend time simply resting in the acknowledged presence of God.

3   How can we become mirrors of Divine perfection? How should worship affect and transform our lives? Does our worship, in church and at home, do that?

16

Freedom and Knowledge

'Thine is the kingdom and the power and the glory for ever.'
(Matthew 6:13; some manuscripts only)

Since the Christian life is one of reflecting God's perfection in ourselves, it is important to think further about the perfection of God, and to see in what ways it can be reflected in us. One way of meditating on God's perfection is to consider each of five basic values, freedom, knowledge, rationality, happiness and co-operation, and ask how they may be found in God. Then we can consider how we may reflect these Divine perfections in ourselves, and so become perfect, as our heavenly Father is perfect.

The freedom of God is his complete independence of any other being. He is the Creator; by his word all things were created. So he does not depend for his existence on anything other than himself. He is self-existent. Nothing can restrict or hamper him at all. He is thus the only wholly free being, the only one that nothing else can interfere with.

However, this makes freedom sound rather negative. God is free from all restrictions. But what is he free to do? The freest being of all will be one who is free to do anything he wills to do; and who wills to do an endlessly creative number of things. So God's freedom is his positive ability to do what he wills. He only has to speak, and creation springs into being. God's freedom is creative – it is a dynamic activity, always realizing values of many different sorts. God is the source of all values, of all good things. The completest freedom is the highest creativeness. This is sometimes called 'omnipotence'. But that is a poor abstract word. What God possesses is supreme creative power, the dynamic power to realize endless numbers of good things.

Since God is the best of all things, he contains an infinity of values in himself. He does not need to create other values outside himself. He is complete in his own nature. Theologians have thought of him as a ceaseless dynamic activity, realizing his own nature in an endless series of worthwhile states, without depending on anything else whatsoever. His creativeness is complete in himself. Thus to understand God's freedom properly would be to understand God's very being. That we can never comprehend. But we can see how part of his freedom is the power to remain unchanged in glory and majesty, without beginning or end.

That is what the biblical prophets see, as they are taken up, in magnificent visions, into the glory of God. Even Moses sees only the fringes of the robe of God, and then he has to be hidden in the crevice of a rock (Exodus 33:22). No human creature can bear the weight of Divine glory. 'Not that anyone has seen the Father except him who is from God,' says Jesus; 'he has seen the Father' (John 6:46). But many of us have felt the power and terror of God, dwarfing us into insignificance as we catch a glimpse of infinite freedom and endless power.

As we reflect on the grandeur and majesty of creation, so we may come to have a sense of the infinity of its Creator. This is not a question of inference from the observed world. The sense of Divine freedom is the direct sense of a reality beyond all limitations. It is that sense which the prophets felt, and of which they speak in images and metaphors. Their words have the impress of infinity; it has grasped them and spoken through them, conveying truths beyond human knowing, in words which convey more than the intellect can ever make explicit. So revelation completes reflection and experience, conveying the idea of the one supreme Creator God in whom alone freedom is complete.

But how can we share in this freedom, the freedom of a God who creates millions of galaxies, who flings out the stars from his fingertips, who holds in being a million million stars and planets? Perfect freedom and endless creativity can belong only to God, the One to whom no other can be likened (Isaiah

40:18). We cannot be told to have such freedom. Dread seems to be the only appropriate feeling in the face of such absolute power, so totally unlike anything else that we know.

The thought of the unlimited power of God may affect our morality both for good and for ill. If belief in God is merely theoretical, any influence will be slight. But if the sense of infinite freedom grasps us and holds us in thrall, it will revolutionize all our attitudes. It may actually undermine our ordinary morality. It may do so by causing us to give up any attempt at independent moral judgement at all. Then we will be slaves of God, or what we take to be God. No bestiality will be too great for one who is the slave of absolute power. Thus religion can dehumanize even as it tries to attain the highest moral eminence. Many modern atheistic writers have been very conscious of this dehumanizing effect. They have thought that religion is bound to undermine morality in this way. But of course that is simply not true. Religion is always a dangerous commodity, and it can have terrible effects on people. But if God is rightly seen, it is a liberating and ennobling power.

The sense of infinite freedom should liberate us from our own limitations and frustrations. Instead of looking for freedom as a freedom to do whatever we want, we will aim to join in and co-operate with the immense creative activity of God. Then we can see the meaning of that obscure-sounding phrase, 'Thy service is perfect freedom'. We can be children, not slaves, gladly serving God out of love and gratitude. We serve him by co-operating in bringing about his creative plans. As we co-operate with him, we discover what real creativity means. Our freedom is extended and enlarged, and we find ourselves capable of doing things we never thought possible. It is when we put ourselves in tune with the creative energies of God that we discover that enormous expansion of capabilities which lets us see what perfect freedom is.

We can enter into the freedom of God, then, by letting God's creative energies work in us, bringing us to new heights of inspiration, strength and activity. This is the power of the Spirit, which coursed through Bezalel as he designed the sanctuary in the wilderness (Exodus 31:1–5); which filled Samson with strength and courage; which inspired the prophets to words filled with more than human insight. When we enter into the freedom of the Spirit, that power becomes ours. Of course we can never be perfectly free, as only God can be. Our perfection is to let ourselves be brought to the full realization of our own limited but God-given capabilities, as we let the Spirit of God work within us. As we do so, the Kingdom which Jesus proclaimed becomes present; God reigns; his Kingdom comes.

The difference between Christian ideas of freedom and the sort of freedom which secular liberalism talks about now becomes clear. I think it is true that post-Enlightenment ideas of freedom and liberty have derived from the Christian gospel. But when they are divorced from that gospel, they take on a new and anarchic spirit. The freedom of the creative Spirit becomes the freedom of total indifference. The philosophy of secular liberalism asks us to extend our freedom, so as to permit all human desires to be maximized. It asks that we should be left alone, to do whatever we wish. But the faith of Christ asks us to become fellow workers with the creative purposes of God. It asks us to conform our desires to those purposes. It asks for our commitment and love, and offers the power of the Spirit to bring our creative abilities to undreamed-of heights.

As the Creator of all things, God knows everything that he has made. He does not only know the externals, as we do. He knows the secrets of every heart, all our hidden thoughts, which we often do not know ourselves. Nor is his knowledge something abstract, as if it was a list of facts. Real knowledge is not just knowing about something. It is a full appreciation of things, in all their uniqueness and particularity. If I know Beethoven's first symphony, I do not just know where all the notes are. I only really know it when I appreciate it, when I love it. Knowledge and love go closely together. I can only know other persons when I love them. So God's knowledge of us is his love of all that we are.

But there is much evil in the world, as well as good. Surely God cannot love and appreciate evil? That would certainly be absurd. But to understand evil, one must still appreciate fully what it is – that it is precisely the frustration of good. One cannot love evil, but one should understand it. One must be able to discriminate exactly what is evil and what is good, how evil can be overcome and destroyed. Even here, then, knowledge means involvement and understanding, which is more than just the ability to state some fact. The two main elements of perfect knowledge are understanding and appreciation of value. God fully understands all things and fully appreciates all values. His knowledge is infinite, because there is nothing that can act as a barrier to it, and nothing that is beyond its reach. It is comprehensive and deep, without error or imperfection.

How can we imitate the perfection of God's knowledge? We can never be omniscient. But we can aim at perfection in knowledge by aiming to avoid ignorance and error, and we can aim to extend our understanding and appreciation of the goodness that is in things. In doing this, we are growing into the likeness of God. A belief in a God of supreme knowledge can again make either a bad or a good difference to our view of morality. We might, if we badly misconceive the truth, think of God as the one who is always watching us, in a judgemental way. He will then seem to be an oppressive tyrant, leaving us no privacy, always watching and ready to condemn. This is the image of God against which Jean-Paul Sartre rebelled so strongly. It is a very unpleasant image. God the Great Snooper is something one might well reject if one can. The worst that can happen is that we begin to do his snooping for him; we try to see into other people's thoughts and control them at all times. So religion becomes repression and thought-control, a malign and powerful cause of terror and human harm.

But we do not have to think of God like that. If we think of him as the One who completely understands us and who appreciates and delights in all that is of unique value about us, that is a much more positive image. Then, as we seek to imitate God, we seek to grow in positive understanding of others, and to delight in what is unique and particular about them. If we see all people as God sees them, we see their positive possibilities, not their faults. The test of whether we are growing in Divine knowledge is whether we understand and enjoy other persons more, precisely because of their difference from us, their own proper uniqueness, created by God to enrich the world by diversity.

To grow in understanding, appreciation and enjoyment of God's world and of the living creatures in it is to grow into the likeness of God. That sounds a rather external thing, as if we are quite different from God, but a bit similar to him. However, the real relation between God and us is much closer. For God is present within our hearts and minds, at the very centre of our selves. As we grow in faith, so we begin to clear away those barriers of ignorance and prejudice which keep us in ignorance of the presence of God. God begins to manifest himself more clearly in us. As the New Testament puts it, the mind of Christ is formed in us. So our quest is to let our minds become channels of the mind of God.

When this happens fully, we can say, with St Paul, 'It is no longer I who live, but Christ who lives in me' (Galatians 2:20). Christ's understanding and loving knowledge begin to take shape in our minds. At last, when we see without prejudice, without the affection that makes us too partial to those we love, and without the hatred that prevents us from understanding others, then we see with the Christ-nature within us. We delight in creation because it is beautiful. We delight in others because they are each of unique and irreplaceable value. We delight in understanding more and more of the natural world. Scientific research and discovery are a growth into the mind of God, as well as the love of beauty which we express in music, painting and poetry. For a Christian, the pursuit of knowledge is not just the accumulation of more and more facts. It is a continual delight in understanding the world in all its beauty and complexity. It is a continual attempt to understand and celebrate the particularity of things – not just abstract concepts and ideas, but the unique unrepeatable presence of each particular, bearing its own specific and precious value.

The prophets' experience of Divine knowledge was their experience of 'being known' by God; being known, being judged and being forgiven. In the presence of God, they felt themselves wholly open to his gaze. But he was always a God of mercy, whose knowledge of the secrets of the heart enabled him to heal and forgive the deepest and most shameful hurts.

The more abstract idea of 'omniscience' developed later, by reflection on what the perfection of God requires. Its root remains the openness of the heart to its Maker. And so the root of human knowledge, too, lies in our striving to see things as they truly are, with compassion and tenderness. That is why knowledge, at its ideal limit, passes into love. And why the greatest of all knowing, our knowledge of God, evokes in us the deepest and truest love, the love of being and its source.

The first three ways in which we can imitate the perfection of God are the striving for creativity, for understanding and for appreciation of all good things. There is no opposition between obedience to God and the pursuit of human fulfilment. For we obey God best precisely by pursuing the fulfilment of the natures which he has given us. In that way, we become like him and achieve our proper goal and end. Christian morality is a deeply humane and person-centred morality. But it broadens our understanding of human nature by setting it clearly in relation to the infinite nature of God who is both its source and its supreme object of desire. When we pray that the Kingdom of God should come, we are praying that his rule should begin in our lives. That rule begins when his unlimited creativeness, understanding and love of goodness take root in our hearts. Then we become, not merely imitators, but instruments of the presence of God in all his fullness of being and perfection.

Questions

1   The creativity of God is seen in the splendour of the stars and of all living things. Does my life share in this creativity? How can I be more creative in the things I do today?

2   Do I take enough trouble to understand the world around me, and the experiences and feelings of other people? How can I understand them in more like the deep and complete way in which God understands them?

3   Do I spend enough time simply delighting in the uniqueness and particularity of things and people? Do I appreciate their value and diversity? Think of a particular person as one in whom Christ is present and can grow, and consider how that growth can be encouraged (and it cannot be compelled!).

17

Wisdom

'If your eye is sound, your whole body will be full of light.'
(Matthew 6:22)

We have seen something of what it means to say that God is
omnipotent and omniscient. The third basic perfection which
God must possess supremely is reason. God made the world
with infinite wisdom, and as scientists come to understand it
more, they appreciate more just how supremely rational its
structure is. Some people have thought that faith and reason
conflict. This may be because of a belief that reason must
work by collecting evidence that will convince anyone beyond
reasonable doubt; and that it must never leap beyond what the
evidence demands. But the evidence available to the senses is
not sufficient to compel belief in God. So there must be a 'leap
of faith', which goes beyond, or even contradicts the demands
of reason.

What we need to counteract this view is a deeper understanding of what rationality is. Human beings are not disinterested
observers of the cosmic scene, who can collect and weigh evidence in a completely objective way. We are participants in a
historical process, with our own needs and interests, our own
points of view within the process. Rationality, in its deepest
sense, is a skill or capacity which involves sensitivity and sound
judgement. In other words, it is a very personal and even
intuitive capacity.

If we want to have a reasonable view about something, we
need to get as much information as possible, select out the
relevant parts of that information, weigh up the relative
strengths of various considerations that come to light, construct

a theory which explains the information as well as possible,
become aware of the chief objections to our own opinions, and
achieve the most balanced and coherent overall account we
can. In doing this very complicated set of things, we do not
follow rules which we have explicitly laid down, and can apply
automatically. It is a much more subtle and creative thing than
that.

It is rather like riding a bicycle. If we had to remember the
rules and apply them consciously, we would fall off. We just
acquire the skill, and some people are better at it than others.
So it is with rationality. We do not have a set of rules which
we consciously apply, to arrive at the correct decision. We
acquire the skills of selection, putting into patterns, weighing
up arguments, sensing possible objections and organizing our
data into a more or less coherent whole. Some people will
always be better at it than others. And some people who are
tremendously good at following rules will never be much good
at making reasonable decisions. They know the rules, but they
may lack the skill to apply them entirely.

The most important skill involved in being reasonable is the
skill of discernment – of seeing what the 'evidence' is and how
to describe it. The extraordinary thing about human life is
that there is no agreement about what the evidence is. Some
philosophers will insist that we can only accept what is directly
apparent to the senses as evidence. They then define what is
apparent to the senses as a set of private sensations. So all
our knowledge has to be somehow inferred from primitive
sensations. People who take this view are not very likely to
find that God looms very large in their thoughts. God will seem
irrational to them.

But why should we take that view? The actual evidence we
have may be much richer and more diverse than just a set of
sensations. Why should the world not be shot through with the
presence of God? Why should we not say that we have evidence
of God in and through all his works, and in his presence to our
minds and hearts? It is not that he is inferred, but that he is
known to be always there, as the source and sustainer of all
things. It is easy to miss that evidence, the evidence of a personal presence at the heart of all things. It is easy to misdescribe

it, and be mistaken about what it is. But that does not mean that there is no such evidence. There may well be such evidence, which only those with the gift of discernment are able to see.

Belief in God will be reasonable if it provides a way of integrating all our experience within a coherent framework which gives it meaning. Of course we can argue about whether it does this or not. Since our human understanding is admittedly very weak, it is most unlikely that we will actually have a perfectly coherent framework. But we might have one which is at least no weaker than any others available to us, and which offers possibilities no other framework can – the possibility of eternal life, happiness and meaning.

There may be a number of more or less reasonable life-views. Reason itself may not be able to decide between them, but why should it? Reason is not some sort of separate faculty which makes all our decisions for us. It is we, as whole persons, with our feelings and goals and commitments, who must decided reasonably or unreasonably. In other words, reason does not tell us what to do. We can use the skills of reason well or badly, as we ourselves decide what to do. So we can see how faith can be seen to complete reason. We must seek to make decisions as reasonably as possible, but in the end it may be most reasonable to make a commitment of faith and trust in a situation where all the facts will never become totally clear. That is the leap of faith. It is not the acceptance of some belief we cannot really justify. It is a commitment of trust which we make once we decide there may be a supremely desirable being, who is the proper object of our unreserved love.

When we make that leap, we do not leave reason behind. Rather, we advance to new depths of wisdom, as love illuminates the world and drives out the illusions and the disguises which our despair and sin project onto it. Once again, the lesson of Jesus is that we see what our eyes let us see. The unsound eye sees a world of darkness; the sound eye fills us with light. What we see depends to a great extent on what we are. Once we are taken into the reason, the wisdom, of God, we see the world behind the veil of appearance, which so often hides it from us. We see that reality is not a collection of

meaningless sensations, strung together in some quite acciden-
tal way. It is the manifestation of the supremely real, the God
whose nature is love. Though it is perverted by evil, by
estrangement from the Creator, when we are inwardly
illumined by the Divine light, we see it as it truly is in the mind
of God.

So when we aim to be reasonable, we are not just trying to
construct good arguments. We are seeking the discerning eye
of wisdom, which sees things truly, weighs them justly and
relates them wisely. We are aiming to become one with Christ,
the wisdom of God, through whom all things were created, and
who is the supreme pattern in the light of which all things are
to be rightly understood.

But is reason really to be trusted? Are the products of human
reason not vain and empty systems of intellectual arrogance
and pretension? Some people distrust reason, thinking that it
excludes feeling or the mysterious depths of a reality beyond
intellect. Certainly, there seems little chance of human beings
framing one clear and precise system which mirrors the universe
as it truly is. Reason *can* exercise a restrictive role, acting as a
supreme arbiter which rules out intuition and the commitment
of faith. On the other hand, to renounce reason is to give
ourselves up to the dark forces of irrational passion and prejudice. It is to be unable to distinguish truth from error, good
from bad. It is to descend to a sub-human level.

The Bible is aware of this ambiguity of reason. It clearly
contrasts the 'wisdom of this world' with the wisdom of God
(1 Corinthians 1:18–25). For the wisdom of this world, the cross
is foolishness. It does not seem to fit into our ideas of what is
proper for God. But the wisdom of God sees deeper, for it
sees that the foundation of the Divine being is love. What is
needed is to think of wisdom properly. If we say the world is
rational, we need not mean that it is one neat and tidy deductive
system, with no loose ends, no mystery, no intuition or feeling.
Its reality may be far beyond human intellectual abilities.
Indeed, most theologians agree that God is beyond human
understanding. But that does not mean he is irrational. He is
beyond our reason, not below it. There is an abyss of creativity
in God, the dazzling darkness which intellect cannot grasp, the

reality beyond name and form which is even beyond being itself, as we understand it. Those who come to know God will know that.

But God is not some arbitrary force or power which is alien to reason. His is the wisdom which shapes the world and which gives to human minds their understanding of things. Wisdom is the power of relating things rightly, making fruitful patterns and comparisons, seeing the interconnectedness of all things. It is also the capacity to see the limits of our intellectual powers, to see where our little systems fail to meet the complexity of things. Wisdom is the power to see where intellect applies and where it must fall silent. It is the capacity to admit the fragility of the intellect. But it will not renounce the claims of intellect where they are in order. Only when infused with Divine power can we gain such wisdom. It is a gift of the Spirit. It is more; it is the working of the Spirit within us. The wisdom of this world looks to gain power over things, to control them by fitting them to our systems of thought. The wisdom of the Spirit seeks to see things as they are, to overcome the ignorance and arrogance which places a barrier between us and the glory of being.

When the prophets saw God as a God of wisdom, they had in mind the marvellous and intricate ways in which his purposes could weave together all human purposes into a pattern aimed at final fulfilment. The wise person aims at good without destroying the freedom of others. So God aims at the fruition of his purpose without destroying human choice. His wisdom is the weaving of all things together for good, to those who love him, who will finally turn to him.

So when we pursue wisdom, we are not seeking to become frightfully clever or intellectual – that might well lead to intellectual arrogance and snobbery. We are seeking a closer knowledge and acceptance of God's purposes, of the ways in which human lives are woven into a pattern which leaves them free but always offers them good. We are seeking to know the limits of our reason, and the skill to see the unity of all things in God, to see the reality behind appearances, to see the relatedness of things in their due proportion, to see the traces of the infinite God in all finite things. We are seeking the ability to interpret the signs of God in all our experiences, and the skill to live well, achieving our proper aim in all the complexity of life. If that is what reason is, we cannot distrust it or oppose it to faith. In seeking it, we are seeking the Divine wisdom, which enables us to see things clearly and place them in due order and proportion. If we would imitate God's perfection, we must seek to be wise. 'The Lord by wisdom founded the earth; by understanding he established the heavens' (Proverbs 3:19). The resolute pursuit of reason is an inescapable Christian ideal.

Questions

1   In what ways can I sense the presence of God in my experiences? How can I deepen this sense and strengthen it?

2   'All things work together for good to those who love God.' How may the wisdom of God use the events of my life for good?

3   Is faith reasonable? How far should I allow reason to shape or determine my faith? Is God beyond the reach of reason?

18

Divine Love

*'Whatever you wish that men would do to you, do so to them;
for this is the law and the prophets.'* (Matthew 7:12)

We have considered how the Christian life is an imitation of
the freedom, knowledge and wisdom of God. In the very first
chapter, we have considered how the Christian life is a sharing
in the joy and happiness of God. These are four of the five
basic values of human morality, raised to their supreme degree
in the one holy Creator of all. The fifth basic value in human
morality is co-operation. When this value is raised to its
supreme degree, it is seen to be the value of love. Jesus teaches
something new and distinctive about the love of God, and so
about how we are to imitate or share in God's love.

If it had not been for Jesus, we might see the perfections of
God in quite a different light. We might see God as a being
whose supreme power is seen in his total control of all that
happens, his all-determining will. His knowledge might be seen
as a remote and intellectual knowledge of all that happens,
unmoved by the suffering or joy of creatures, but preventing
them from ever escaping from his control. His rationality could
be seen as an unemotional process of cold calculation, uncon-
cerned with the petty things of this small planet. His happiness
could be seen as a bliss which remains undisturbed by any harm
or evil that happens in creation. And his love might seem, at
best, a compassion or pity for creatures which cannot become
involved in their everyday imperfect affairs. We might, as philosophers like Aristotle have done, think of God as so perfect
that he cannot be involved in an imperfect world at all. Blissful
and all-knowing, he would be without action or involvement in

the world, a perfection as remote from us as anything could ever be.

Jesus' picture of God is quite different. Partly this is because he belongs to the Jewish tradition, which gives a much more positive evaluation to the created world than many other religious traditions. Many religious views think that the best thing for humans is to obtain release from the wheel of rebirth in the world. But the biblical view is that the world is created good, and we are to find our fulfilment within it. Action and creation have a very positive value in the Bible. The prophets of Israel typically found God in the events of history and in the moral demand for justice in society which they felt. They had a keen sense of a moral purpose in human history, and they felt themselves called to proclaim this purpose for their people.

In the Bible, morality, society and history are all given great religious importance. God is seen as a dynamic will, with a purpose for people to carry out. In consequence, he is not seen so much as the unmoving centre of the self, as he is in some other religious traditions, but as the glorious Lord of history, working his purpose out in judgement and mercy. It is the great strength of the teaching of Jesus that he holds both these insights together. He speaks both of the inward quest for perfection, and of the need to pursue the moral purpose of God in history.

In speaking of both these things, he also adds a distinctively new element, which could not at that time be held within the bounds of Judaism. The prophets had felt the Divine power in the events of their history; they had shared in the creative joy of artistic inspiration and strength; they had sensed the judgement and mercy of God on their failures and confessions of wrongdoing. Their concept of God was of a Being wholly other, sole Creator, fearful in majesty, dreadful in power, before whom total submission was the only possible response. 'I repent in dust and ashes,' said Job, all his anger and questionings annihilated in the presence of Almighty Power (Job 42:6). This is a view which is represented quite strongly in the Hebrew Bible, the Old Testament.

What did Jesus add to it? Three elements stand out. First,

there is the idea of the incarnation of God. Of course, we have no way of knowing what Jesus' own conception of the incarnation might have been. But he clearly taught that 'God is love'; and that love is shown in actions of humble service – washing feet, healing disease, being prepared to die if it would help to bring people to God. Jesus' life is the picture of God's love, and the Gospels portray Jesus as knowing that to be the case. If, when God expresses his being in human form, he takes the form of a servant, that says something new and strange about the power of God. It means that God's power is not shown in some sort of tyranny or remote control. It is shown in a love which patiently endures, so as to draw all things to itself. The power of God does not obliterate the wills of human beings. We often find that very strong men are very gentle, because they do not need to prove anything to anyone. So God, needing to prove nothing and having unsurpassable power, acts with supreme gentleness to go on attracting us to love, despite all we do to reject him.

The idea of Divine power is much more positive than the idea of being free from attachment and pain. It involves being free to create and to realize many sorts of good purposes. But it is a power which always gives creatures freedom, and which will never stop drawing them towards perfect love. It is a power which is able even to take pain and suffering into itself, so as to transform them into good. *God is love, and perfect love will use its strength to enlarge the freedom of those it loves, not to compel them into submission*.

The second element Christ adds to the idea of God is that of atonement, of God suffering on the cross for human sin. It is important to see that it is God himself who suffers. He suffers, because suffering is the natural consequence of selfishness and that rejection of love which is sin. God does not need to suffer, since he is perfect love and without sin. But he takes on himself the suffering which is the result of human sin. When the sinless Christ dies on the cross, we see in a direct and appalling way the consequence of our own sin. We see that we injure not only ourselves and others, but that we injure even God, who makes himself vulnerable to our sin. God gave us freedom, and he takes the consequences of our misuse of freedom. The worst that we can do, we do to him. The cross shows what hatred does to love. But it also has healing power; it shows what love can do with hatred. When we see the cost of our sin, it may be too much to bear. But Christ pays that cost, and so assures us that God will accept us if only we trust in him.

The idea of sacrifice is almost universal in religion. It is the idea of giving something to God to express our gratitude and obedience, to establish a firm relationship with him. The Christian gospel teaches that God gives himself to us, so that we will have a perfect offering to unite us to him for ever, and eradicate everything that holds us back from him. God himself is our Saviour and Redeemer. The bliss of God is not untouched by the world's misery. It enters into that misery, but transforms it by the infinite joy that lies in the heart of God. Just as God's power is seen in the patient service of love, so God's joy is seen in the patient enduring of pain, which is taken up into the victory of resurrection. *God is love, and perfect love will seek to bear the suffering of the one it loves.*

The third main element which Christ adds to the idea of God is the insight that, as we are taken into unity in Christ, so we are made sharers in the nature of God itself. God is no longer wholly other and apart from us. We are parts of God; for just as the Son is one with the Father, so we are one in the Son (John 17:11). The Christian vision of God is not of one absolute seamless unity. The doctrine of the Trinity, that God is Three-in-One, shows that God is not some sort of solitary and lonely self-sufficient being. Even in his own inmost being there is an analogy of that relationship of mutual sharing and giving between persons which gives human life its deepest meaning.

One theme which is absolutely central to the Jewish tradition is that you cannot love God if you do not love other people. John writes: 'If anyone says, "I love God", and hates his brother, he is a liar' (1 John 4:20). Jesus stresses that we must love even our enemies. And he sums up the law of love in what has been called the Golden Rule: 'Whatever you wish that men would do to you, do so to them; for this is the law and the prophets.' You can always take this in a stupid way. You can say 'I wish everybody would give me all their money', and then try to give all your money to everybody. Or if you are a policeman, you might have to let criminals get away, because that is what they want you to do to them. Jesus is offering a rule of thumb, not an absolute principle. But it is a very important rule of thumb. It really means that you should treat other people – all other people – as you would like to be treated, with care and consideration. It means that you should try to think of their interests as much as you would think of your own. You should help them to achieve their hopes and ambitions as much as you try to achieve your own.

It would be a great mistake to think that love is always a matter of giving to others, of never thinking of yourself at all. It is good to give to others, there is no doubt about that. But it is not the highest sort of love. Just think of a society in which everyone was always trying to give to everyone else, and nobody ever wanted to receive anything from anybody else. What a frustrating thing it would be, trying to give things to people who either didn't want them, or who immediately gave them to somebody else. The fact is that we like people to accept and enjoy what we have to give them. We like them to value our gifts and be pleased about them. One of the most important things about loving is the ability to receive what others have to give. If we can't do that, it probably means that we don't really think other people have anything worthwhile to give us. So it means that we don't really find them of any great value.

If we really love somebody, we will be glad to accept whatever they give us, just because they give it. What has sometimes gone wrong with 'charity' is that it is always a matter of the richer giving to the poorer. So it makes the poorer feel inferior, and the rich feel as if they are very virtuous for giving away what was only theirs on trust from God in the first place. A relationship of real love is one of taking as well as giving. In accepting that others have something of real value to give, you show love, because you show that you value them as unique persons. For the Christian, this is especially true, since 'we love because God first loved us' (1 John 4:19). We have to receive the love of God; we have to enjoy it and take pleasure in it. So proper human loving begins with accepting, not with giving.

Only when we have been filled with love, will we have enough to let it overflow to others. We can only give what we've got. And only the infinite love of God is enough for us to give to others.

It is not quite right, then, to say, as people sometimes do, that the Christian life is one of total self-giving. A good loving relationship is when two people enjoy one another's company. It is not when each one is just trying to make the other happy. It is when each is made happy by accepting what the other has to give. Of course the greatest test of love is giving up your life for another. Then self-sacrifice is a great virtue. But you make that sacrifice, if you have to, so that someone else can be saved from harm. If you care about their happiness, then the best way of making someone you love, and who loves you, happy is by telling them how much they have to give you. Real love is a matter of receiving as well as giving. The ideal Christian life would be one, not of total self-giving, but of a mutual sharing in a common love. That idea of love, as a positive dynamic and enlivening power, is what the Christian idea of the Trinity tries to express. *God is love, and perfect love will seek to share its life with others.* So God will seek to draw others into his mutual life of giving and receiving.

St Augustine drew a picture of the Trinity in which he suggested that the Father is the lover and the source of love, the Son is the beloved and the image of love, and the Spirit is the love which binds them together in unrestricted mutuality. It is only a picture. But it is one way of conveying the point that God is not some sort of supreme egoist, absorbed in himself. He is the highest form of loving relationship, existing in a way we cannot fully comprehend intellectually.

The Christian gospel is that we are called to live in that love. We are not just told to love other people. We are not just told to imitate God's love. We are offered the being of God himself, which *is* love. First we are shown the love of the Father, in the person of Jesus. Then the Spirit begins to live within us, and takes us into that communion between Father and Son which is supreme love. That is the final aim of the Christian life: to be Spirit-filled, fashioned in the image of the Son in loving adoration of the Father.

The five basic values which form the basis of all reflective human morality are totally transformed by this promise and this vision. The Christian God is not a remote all-knowing and unchanging bliss. We see, perhaps for the first time, what our basic values really are, when they are taken to their supreme degree and rooted in the God who is disclosed in the person of Jesus Christ. Everyone wants happiness. But the follower of Christ is promised eternal life, a joy that no man can ever take away. Everyone desires knowledge. But the follower of Christ is promised the vision of God, and a share in his understanding and appreciation of all created things. Everyone wants to be reasonable. But the follower of Christ is promised a share in the wisdom of God, which sees all things in their due pattern and proportion. Everyone wants freedom. But the follower of Christ is promised the creative power and energy which brings human nature to its true fulfilment. Everyone wants some co-operation. But the follower of Christ is promised a life which is taken up into an endless and unrestricted love. In this way human ideals are transfigured by union with God, who is their source, and human perfection is seen to be, beyond any natural human expectation, a sharing in the perfection of God.

Questions

1 How does the belief that God took the form of a servant in Christ affect our understanding of God's power? What does it mean for the way we exercise power over others – our children, families or employees?

2 How do I understand the sacrifice of Christ for me? What does it tell me about how I am to act towards others – those who suffer or those who are filled with hatred and anger?

3 'Perfect love will seek to share its life.' Do I let others know that I value what they give me? That I can see their lives as a gift to me? How far am I prepared to share my life with them?

19

Light

'You are the light of the world.' (Matthew 5:14)

The Christian gospel assumes that there is a natural knowledge of what is right and wrong, available to anyone who seriously thinks about it. That knowledge depends in no way upon revelation. In one sense, faith in God is quite distinct from having moral beliefs. From a Christian point of view, the whole aim of human life is to love God and enjoy him for ever. If we miss that aim, then, however good we are, we have simply missed the mark, the target of human life. That is what is meant by saying that good works without faith still leaves us in sin. Sin just is missing the mark of human life, missing its main aim and goal. You can live a good life, but if you are still separated from God, not knowing him or loving him above all, you miss your central aim.

Believing in God, really believing, is rather like getting married. The point of getting married is not to be good. It is to enter into a human relationship which is of enormous value; which, for some people, can both bring great happiness and enrich one's character in many ways. It is one thing to be good. It is quite another to have one's whole life transformed by a love which seems to make the whole world glow. The awareness of God brings us into a relationship of love which adds another dimension to the whole of life. Those who have experienced that dimension will always know that 'being good' is not what faith is about; that it can even distract attention from life's greatest value.

That sounds as though faith leaves morality unchanged, whereas it is quite clear that it does not. There are those who revere morality for its own sake. And there are those who just love other people as they are. There is a nobility of spirit in this, but also a deep and irremovable arbitrariness. For why should one respect the moral law or human dignity? One may say that one just should, and that is that! But is there a good reason to respect such petty, misguided lumps of clay on the edge of an insignificant galaxy? The most sensitive and intelligent minds may come to feel that, in the end, whatever values one is theoretically committed to, it does not much matter what human animals, those chance consequences of countless mistakes in genetic replication, do. To place a supreme value on moral rectitude in a universe of infinite caprice may come to seem a final mad cry of arrogance, rather than a precious moral insight.

What is needed to prevent this collapse of moral vision is a strong sense of the presence and love of God. If we believe there is a Being of supreme value who has created all things, who has created us so that we might find fulfilment and happiness by loving him for ever, then we have good reason to obey his will. For there is then a fulfilment to be attained, a purpose to be worked out, a value to respect and revere which is imperishable and incorruptible.

Humanism is the creed that human beings are just worthy of respect in themselves. That says something very true and important. It is a devastating criticism of forms of religion which have treated human persons as mere objects, subservient to some authoritarian creed or set of rules. Yet at its heart there is an element of unrealism. Who among us has not felt at times that human persons are depraved and corrupt, weak and useless? As Sartre put it, 'Man is a useless passion'. Why should we invest so much worth in these petty, egotistical, spiteful and arrogant organisms?

The best answer would be: because they are made in the image of God, for an eternal destiny. The theist is devoted to a being who really is of unsurpassable and changeless worth. That being is absolutely worthy of respect. And God offers us love as our proper destiny. What the Christian gospel does is to place before us a positive vision of human nature and destiny. That vision gives morality a central place in human life.

It becomes part of the ardent desire to love God and help to realize his purposes. It becomes the attempt to regard others with the love of God, to see them in the light of what he intends them to be. It is that vision which makes other people, however degraded and evil they seem, objects of unlimited respect and concern.

An atheist can know what is right, know that it is right to do to others as you would have them do to you, to love your neighbour as yourself. And it is quite possible for an atheist, just as well as a theist, to do what is right. You do not have to be religious to be good. Indeed, humanists have rightly protested that some forms of religion help to corrupt morality. Christian Churches can be obscurantist, legalistic and judge-mental of others. They can promote a hidden sort of self-interest, an interest in 'my salvation'. By contrast, the best humanists promote a humane, tolerant and self-critical ethic which puts many Christians to shame.

For that reason alone, it is impossible to say that *any* sort of religion is better than any sort of atheism. That would be absolutely false. But it is only fair to point out that atheism can also undermine any idea of human dignity; it can under-mine morality itself and lead to the view that since God is dead, everything is permitted. That sort of atheism is probably worse than obscurantist religion, which at least does preserve a notion of human dignity and worth, however shortsighted it may be about seeing the true implications of its own beliefs.

What Christianity adds to the best humanism is that it makes ordinary human nature transparent to the supreme and immu-table value of God. Human persons are worthy of infinite respect. But Christ adds another dimension to human person-hood. He unites it to Divinity, to a love and a value that can never be defeated. This makes a tremendous difference to those who cannot see the point of morality at all, who think it is perhaps just a set of social conventions or personal preferences. God sets before human beings an eternal destiny; he calls them to fulfilment by being filled with his love. We cannot then say that morality is just convention. It has to be the pathway to love. It is rooted in the nature of reality at its deepest level. It becomes a positive and binding duty to pursue its claims with all one's energy. It is rooted in response to a Being of infinite love, and it promises the deepest happiness and fulfilment to us and to the persons who are the objects of our concern. What a total difference from the depressing idea that it is just what other people want to impose on us!

Giving up belief in God can give a sense of freedom and adventure to people who have only seen religion as cramping and oppressive. How sad that the ultimate liberation that Christ offers should ever be seen like that! Jesus' harshest words were reserved for religious people. They were responsible for his death. Perhaps some of his 'religious' followers now are still crucifying the God they claim, and tragically believe themselves, to follow faithfully. The freedom atheism gives is just the freedom to be left alone. True freedom is the revitalizing of human energy and ability that comes when you fall in love. When you fall in love with God, then you are truly free. That is the transformation Christ offers, as he brings God's love close to us. The Christian should gently put this question to the humanist: is humanist morality not in reality a dim afterglow of the love of God? Do duties not exist only to remind us of the things that love, were it fully alive, would gladly and spontaneously do? Of course, if people genuinely believe there is no God, it is good that they should aim to do what is right for its own sake. But even the atheist might see that, if there was a God of supreme love, goodness would be suffused by love. Respect for duty would become part of a deeper love for God, his unsurpassable value, beauty, majesty and love. Morality would indeed be fulfilled and brought to perfection by the revelation of the nature of God in the person of Jesus Christ.

Christ takes our natural knowledge of goodness and deepens it by showing its true foundation in the nature of God. What difference does this make? It changes the vision of what 'love of your neighbour' is. For the Christian, every neighbour, every person, is a soul of unique and irreplaceable value, born to enjoy an eternal life of response to, and sharing in, God's love. All its sufferings can be positively taken up into a deeper fulfilment. All its values take on an added dimension, as they lead out into the unlimited value of God. All its experiences take on meaning as part of a continually growing pattern which is its unique story in relation to God. And all its hopes will have a fulfilment beyond earthly death. The neighbour is essentially a child of God, always in relation to the Father of all, and that relationship defines its innermost character.

Once we see what a human person really is, we can learn how to love it in the most fitting way. The most obvious difference this makes is that we will see each soul as having an interior ideal set before it. In detail, that ideal will be unique to every individual. It will conform to no general pattern, but it will be a goal only that person can know and reach. But in its general outline the goal will be that of union with God and with all those who love God – membership of the Kingdom which Jesus declared to be close at hand to all who heard his teaching with open hearts. This ideal gives a positive vision for every human life. It is not just a minimal standard to be maintained, but the stimulus to an infinite journey towards perfection. The ideal is binding on everyone, for it is placed before people at the very moment of their creation. It is not a matter of personal choice or decision. It is to be realized in the eternal presence of God. So the gospel shows the goal of human life and action; it is *revelatory*.

Then the gospel shows the way to achieve this goal; it is *exemplary*. In Christ, the way is shown to the overcoming of self, the way of losing one's will in the will of God. Morality becomes, not an end in itself, but a response to God's gift and disclosure of himself. If Christ is our pattern, the pattern of our lives, then the reason we should do right is not only that it *is* right, but that God has made this the way to the goal of completed love.

Finally, the gospel shows the means to union with God; it is *charismatic*. It teaches that the gift of God's love in the life and death of Jesus is made available to us through the life and sacraments of the Church, and through the presence of the Spirit within our hearts. All we have to do is turn from self and accept Christ. Morality becomes, not a matter of constant effort, but a matter of constant acceptance, of letting go and allowing God's gift of love to be poured into our lives.

Jesus says 'You are the light of the world'. He does not set before us a universal moral code, which he expects all people to follow. He calls us to be disciples, to live in total commitment to him. The little community of the spirit is not one that should parade its piety or religiosity before the world. Yet it should be like salt, giving flavour to the societies in which it lives. It should be like a lamp, which does not call attention to itself, but illumines everything around it. It is to be distinguished by its unselfish love; by the quiet flourishing of the fruits of patience, peace, kindness, active goodness and joy. In these communities the Kingdom comes; God's future is made present, and God himself is known as a living and active presence. For the light of the world is Christ himself (John 8:12), and the Christian community is set apart to be the vehicle and instrument of his life. We only have to open the shutters of our hearts and let the light shine, to let our selves become transparent to the Self of all. If we could do that consistently and all the time, morality would cease to be important, for we should blaze with the love of God. Morality exists because of the hardness of our hearts. Since our hearts are hard, we must obey its dictates. But we should always hold before our eyes that vision which Christ places before us, which fulfils morality and shows its innermost meaning, which draws our fractured lives into the eternal joy of God.

'And when Jesus finished these sayings, the crowds were astonished at his teaching, for he taught them as one who had authority' (Matthew 7:28).

Questions

1 How does belief in a living God affect my view of morality? How is my faith in God related to my practice of morality? Does it make it more rigid and restrictive, or more active and effective?

2 Does my religious faith help me to respect others and value them? Or does it lock me into a little world of pious practices with people who think like me? How can I make it more outward-looking? Use Matthew 25 to reflect on Jesus' words about faith.

3 Is my church a light of unselfish love in the local

community? Can neighbours and strangers find there a fore-shadowing of joy in the Kingdom of God, the rule of love?

Bibliography

These are just a few recent books which provide scholarly analyses of the sermon. I am most grateful to Professor Morna Hooker, of Cambridge University, and Professors Graham Stanton and Leslie Houlden, of King's College, London University, for their great but largely unknowing help in my own studies. I do not hold them responsible, however, for any of the views expressed here.

H. K. McArthur, *Understanding the Sermon on the Mount*, 1960.
J. Jeremias, *The Sermon on the Mount*, 1961.
W. S. Kissinger, *The Sermon on the Mount: a History of Interpretation and Bibliography*, 1975.
R. A. Guelich, *The Sermon on the Mount: a Foundation for Understanding*, 1982.
H. Hendrickx, *The Sermon on the Mount*, 1984.
H. D. Betz, *Essays on the Sermon on the Mount*, 1985.
J. Lambrecht, *The Sermon on the Mount*, 1985.
G. Strecker, *The Sermon on the Mount: an Exegetical Commentary*, 1988.